Unicorns, dragons

AND MORE FANTASY AMIGURUMI 3

Unicorns, Dragons and more Fantasy Amigurumi 3
Bring 14 Wondrous Characters to Life!

Second print run, February 2024

First published September 2023 by
Meteoor BV, Antwerpen, Belgium
www.meteoorbooks.com
hello@meteoorbooks.com

Text and images
© 2023 Meteoor BV (BE0550756201) and designers

Have you made characters with patterns from
this book? Share your creations on
www.amigurumi.com/4400
or on Instagram with #fantasyamigurumi3

Pictures by Studio Flits & Flash (www.flitsenflash.be)
Printed and bound by Grafistar

ISBN 978-949164-349-1
D/2023/13.531/3

A catalogue record for this book is available
from the Royal Library of Belgium.

Unicorns, dragons

AND MORE FANTASY AMIGURUMI 3

BRING 14 WONDROUS CHARACTERS TO LIFE!

METEOOR BOOKS

CONTENTS

Hi there!

Choose your favorite crochet hook, wave it around with
a flourish and say the magic words with me: 'Unicorns, Dragons
and More Fantasy Amigurumi 1, 2 … 3'! That's right, the most
enchanting amigurumi series continues in this third bedazzling
book. There's something truly magical about transforming a
simple strand of yarn into a toy and we can't wait to see your
crochetwork sparkle!

There's always a new adventure to be found in this world of
wonder, but beware, things may not be quite as they seem …
Take Morgana, for example. She looks like a cute seal, but she's
actually a selkie who loves town festivals and a good shot of
Scottish whiskey. Maisie the Kraken may have a fearsome
family, but for now she's just a baby playing with her paper
boats. Alwyn the Wizard looks wise, but he accidentally
enlarged his family's cat by threefold, with no one able
to shrink the cat down for hours.

Beginners as well as advanced crocheters can conjure up these
wondrous characters with a flick of their hooks. All patterns
are accompanied by easy-to-follow instructions as well as
explanations of all stitches used, and are easily customizable, so
it's a small step to dream up your very own fantasy amigurumi!

Perhaps the most magical thing about amigurumi is the
community it creates. Have you made a character and do you want
to share your work and passion with your fellow crochet wizards?
We'd love to see your photos on *www.amigurumi.com/4400*
or on Instagram with *#fantasyamigurumi3*.

We wish you a lot of fun crocheting!

BASIC MATERIALS

COLORFUL YARN

For every pattern in this book, we've listed the yarn used to create the design. Don't feel tied to these yarn choices though: any weight of cotton, acrylic or wool can be used as a substitute. If you change the yarn weight (thickness), you'll want to match the right crochet hook accordingly. Check the chart below for a quick comparison of yarn weights and corresponding recommended hook sizes.

The patterns don't state the yarn quantity. The amounts are rather small and will vary according to how loosely or tightly you crochet. You could use the remnants of other projects or start with a new ball of yarn. When more than one 50g ball is needed, we mention this in the materials list.

CROCHET HOOK

Hooks as well come in different sorts and sizes. Bigger hooks make bigger stitches than smaller ones. It's important to match the right hook size with the right weight of yarn. For amigurumi, you generally want to use a hook two or three sizes smaller than what is recommended on your yarn label. The crochet fabric should be quite tight, without any gaps through which the stuffing can escape. Using a smaller hook makes it easier to achieve this.

Hooks are usually made from aluminum or steel. Metal hooks tend to slip between the stitches more easily. Preferably choose a crochet hook with a rubber ergonomic handle.

STITCH MARKER

A stitch marker is a small metal or plastic clip. It's a simple tool to mark your starting point and give you the assurance that you've made the right number of stitches in each round. Mark the last stitch of the round with your stitch marker. You move your stitch marker up one round at the end of each round. When you reach your stitch marker after crocheting a new round, you take it out, crochet in this stitch, then put it in the last stitch you crocheted.

STUFFING

For the filling, polyester fiberfill is advised. It is wash-

NUMBER (SYMBOL)	1	2	3	4	5	6
CATEGORY NAME	super fine	fine	light	medium	heavy	very heavy
UK YARN TYPE	3 ply	4 ply	double knitting (DK)	aran	chunky	super chunky
US YARN TYPE	Fingering	Sport	Light Worsted	Worsted	Bulky	Extra Bulky
THE HOOK WE RECOMMEND IN US SIZE	8 steel to B-1	B-1	B-1 to E-4	E-4 to 7	7 to I-9	I-9 to K-10 1/2
THE HOOK WE RECOMMEND IN METRIC SIZE	1.5 to 2.5mm	2.5mm	2.5 to 3.5mm	3.5 to 4.5mm	4.5 to 5.5mm	5.5 to 6.5mm

able and non-allergenic. The individual parts of a toy are stuffed while the piece is being crocheted. The stuffing of wider pieces such as the head or body begins when they are roughly half finished. For stuffing very thin pieces in which you cannot fit a finger, the back of a crochet hook or a chopstick can be used. Generally, when stuffing a toy, it's important to use more stuffing than you might initially think. If the toy is not stuffed tightly, it will lose its shape over time. On the other hand, if it's overstuffed, the stuffing may cause the fabric to stretch and become visible. You'll need to find the right balance.

SAFETY EYES

For most designs, safety eyes are used. Safety eyes come in two different parts — the front (the bead that will show on the outside, on a ribbed stem) and the back (the washer). The washer keeps the eye in place. Be careful when you apply safety eyes: once you put the washer on, you won't be able to pull it off again, so make sure that the post is where you want it to be before attaching the washer.

If you're crocheting these toys for children under the age of three, it is advised to embroider the facial features for safety.

TAPESTRY NEEDLE

For embroidery, a tapestry needle with a rounded tip is used. This rounded tip makes it easier to insert your needle in a specific space without splitting your yarn.

SEWING PINS

It can be handy to have some sewing pins lying around, to help position body parts before sewing them on permanently.

WHAT YOU SHOULD KNOW BEFORE YOU START

SKILL LEVEL

easy (✶)
intermediate (✶ ✶)
advanced (✶ ✶ ✶)

Every pattern is marked with a skill level to indicate how easy they are to make. If this is your first time making amigurumi, it's best to start with an easy pattern and work up to the intermediate and advanced ones.

AMIGURUMI GALLERY

With each pattern, we have included a URL and QR code that will take you to that character's dedicated online gallery. Share your finished amigurumi, find inspiration in the color and yarn choices of your fellow crocheters and enjoy the fun of crocheting.

Simply follow the link or scan the QR code with your mobile phone. Phones with iOS will scan the QR code automatically in camera mode. For phones with Android you may need to activate QR code scanning or install a separate QR Reader app.

PATTERN STRUCTURE

- These patterns are worked in continuous spirals. Crocheting in spirals can be confusing since there's no clear indication of where a new round begins and the previous one ends. To keep track of the rounds, you can mark the end of a round with a stitch marker or safety pin. After crocheting the next round, you should end up right above your stitch marker. Move your stitch marker at the end of each round to keep track of where you are.
- At the beginning of each line you will find 'Rnd + a number' to indicate which round you are in.
- If a round is repeated, you'll read 'Rnd 9 – 12', for example. You then repeat this round four times,

crocheting the stitches in round 9, 10, 11 and 12.
- Although we usually crochet in rounds, occasionally it happens that we switch to rows, going back and forth instead of working in continuous spirals. When we switch to rows, it will be indicated with 'Row + a number'. You end the row with a ch 1 and turn your crochetwork to start the next. Don't count this turning chain as a stitch and skip it when working the next row (unless otherwise mentioned).
- We sometimes work in joined rounds, closing the round with a slst in the first st and ch 1. When working in joined rounds, we make the first stitch of the next round in the same stitch where we made the slst.
- At the end of each line you will find the number of stitches you should have in square brackets, for example [9]. When in doubt, take a moment to check your stitch count.
- When parts of the instructions repeat throughout the round, we place them between rounded brackets, followed by the number of times this part should be worked. We do this to shorten the pattern and make it less cluttered.

STITCH TUTORIALS

If this is your first time making amigurumi, you might find it useful to have a tutorial at hand. With the stitches explained on these pages, you can make all of the amigurumi in this book. We suggest you practice the basic stitches before you start making one of the designs. This will help you to read the patterns and abbreviations more comfortably, without having to browse back to these pages. This book is written in US crochet terms.

TUTORIAL VIDEOS

With each stitch explanation we have included a URL and QR code that will take you to our online stitch tutorial video, showing the technique step by step to help you master it even more quickly. Simply follow the link or scan the QR code with your smartphone. Phones with iOS will scan the QR code automatically in camera mode. For phones with Android you may need to install a QR Reader app first.

CHAIN (abbreviation: ch)

If you're working in rows, your first row will be a series of chain stitches.
Step 1: Use the hook to draw the yarn through the loop.
Step 2: Pull the loop until tight.
Step 3: Wrap the yarn over the hook from back to front. Pull the hook, carrying the yarn, through the loop already on your hook. You have now completed one chain stitch.
Step 4: Repeat these steps as indicated in the pattern to create a foundation chain.

Scan or visit
www.stitch.show/ch
for the video tutorial

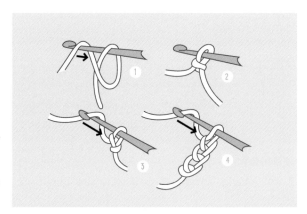

INSERT THE HOOK
(PLACEMENT OF STITCHES)

With the exception of chains, all crochet stitches require the hook to be inserted in existing stitches. Insert the hook underneath both top loops of the stitch in the row or round below. When inserting the hook, you take it from front to back through a stitch. The point of the hook must always look down or sideways, so the hook doesn't snag the yarn or the fabric.

When asked to crochet FLO or BLO you make the same stitch but leave one loop untouched.

Inserting the hook in front loops only
(abbreviation: FLO)

When working in Front Loops Only, you pick up only the front loop toward you.

Inserting the hook in back loops only
(abbreviation: BLO)

When working in Back Loops Only, you pick up only the back loop away from you.

Scan or visit
**www.stitch.show/
FLO-BLO** for the
video tutorial

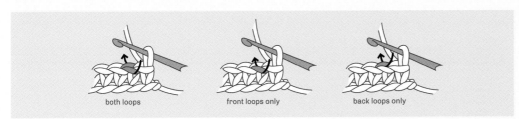

both loops   front loops only   back loops only

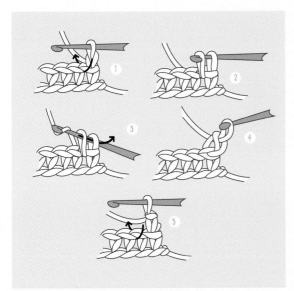

SINGLE CROCHET (abbreviation: sc)

Single crochet is the stitch that will be most frequently used in this book.

Step 1: Insert the hook into the next stitch.

Step 2: Wrap the yarn over the hook. Pull the yarn through the stitch. You will see that there are now two loops on the hook.

Step 3: Wrap the yarn over the hook again and draw it through both loops at once.

Step 4: You have now completed one single crochet.

Step 5: Insert the hook into the next stitch to continue.

Scan or visit
www.stitch.show/sc
for the video tutorial

Scan or visit
www.stitch.show/slst
for the video tutorial
↓

SLIP STITCH (abbreviation: slst)

A slip stitch is used to move across one or more stitches at once or to finish a piece.

Step 1: Insert your hook into the next stitch.

Step 2: Wrap the yarn over the hook and draw through the stitch and loop on your hook at once.

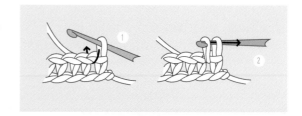

HALF DOUBLE CROCHET (abbreviation: hdc)

Step 1: Bring your yarn over the hook from back to front before placing the hook in the stitch.

Step 2: Wrap the yarn over the hook and draw the yarn through the stitch. You now have three loops on the hook.

Step 3: Wrap the yarn over the hook again and pull it through all three loops on the hook. You have completed your first half double crochet.

Step 4: To continue, bring your yarn over the hook and insert it in the next stitch.

Scan or visit
www.stitch.show/hdc
for the video tutorial
↓

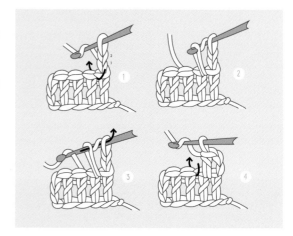

DOUBLE CROCHET (abbreviation: dc)

Step 1: Bring your yarn over the hook from back to front before placing the hook in the stitch.

Step 2: Wrap the yarn over the hook and draw the yarn through the stitch. You now have three loops on the hook.

Step 3: Wrap the yarn over the hook again and pull it through the first two loops on the hook. You now have two loops on the hook.

Step 4: Wrap the yarn over the hook one last time and draw it through both loops on the hook. You have now completed one double crochet.

Step 5: To continue, bring your yarn over the hook and insert it in the next stitch.

Scan or visit
www.stitch.show/dc
for the video tutorial
↓

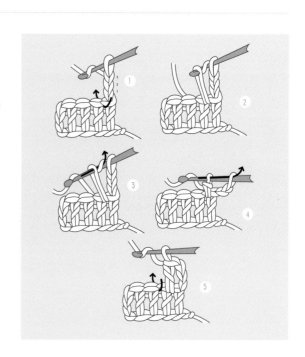

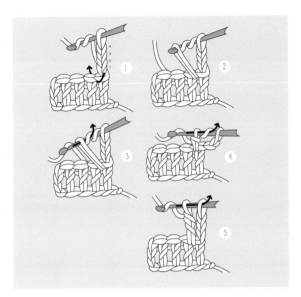

TRIPLE CROCHET (abbreviation: tr)

Step 1: Bring your yarn over the hook twice from back to front before placing the hook in the stitch.

Step 2: Wrap the yarn over the hook and draw the yarn through the stitch. You now have four loops on the hook.

Step 3: Wrap the yarn over the hook again and pull it through the first two loops on the hook. You now have three loops on the hook.

Step 4: Wrap the yarn over the hook again and pull it through the first two loops on the hook. You now have two loops on the hook.

Step 5: Wrap the yarn over the hook one last time and pull it through both loops on the hook. You have now completed one triple crochet.

Step 6: To continue, bring your yarn over the hook twice and insert it in the next stitch.

Scan or visit
www.stitch.show/tr
for the video tutorial

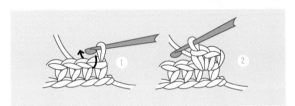

INCREASE (abbreviation: inc)

To increase, two single crochet stitches are made in the same stitch. This way, new stitches are created and the piece expands.

Step 1: Make a first single crochet stitch in the next stitch.

Step 2: Make a second single crochet stitch in the same stitch.

Scan or visit
www.stitch.show/inc
for the video tutorial

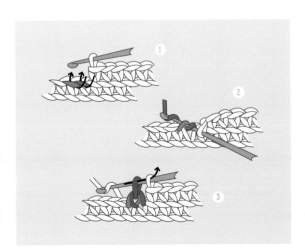

INVISIBLE DECREASE (abbreviation: dec)

When decreasing, two stitches are crocheted together. The number of stitches in a round therefore decreases and the piece shrinks.

Step 1: Insert the hook in the front loop of your first stitch. Now immediately insert your hook in the front loop of the second stitch. You now have three loops on your hook.

Step 2: Wrap the yarn over the hook and pull it through the first two loops on the hook.

Step 3: Wrap the yarn over the hook again and pull it through the remaining two loops on the hook. You have now completed one invisible decrease.

Scan or visit
www.stitch.show/dec
for the video tutorial

HALF DOUBLE CROCHET DECREASE
(abbreviation: hdc dec)

Step 1: Bring your yarn over the hook from back to front before placing the hook in the next stitch.

Step 2: Wrap the yarn over the hook and pull it through the stitch. You now have three loops on your hook. Repeat this from the start in the next stitch. You now have five loops on your hook.

Step 3: Wrap the yarn over your hook once more and draw it through all five loops on your hook. You have now decreased two half double crochet stitches.

Scan or visit
www.stitch.show/hdcdec
for the video tutorial

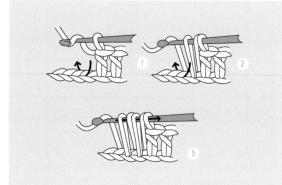

CROCHET AROUND A FOUNDATION CHAIN
Some pieces start with an oval. You make an oval by crocheting around a foundation chain.

Step 1: Crochet a foundation chain with as many chains as mentioned in the pattern and skip the first chain on the hook.

Step 2-3: Work a sc stitch in the next chain stitch. Work your crochet stitches into each chain across as mentioned in the pattern.

Step 4: The last stitch before turning is usually an increase stitch.

Step 5: Turn your work upside down to work into the underside of the chain stitches. You'll notice that only one loop is available, simply insert your hook in this loop. Work your stitches into each chain across.

Step 6: When finished, your last stitch should be next to the first stitch you made. You can now continue working in spirals.

Scan or visit
www.stitch.show/oval
for the video tutorial

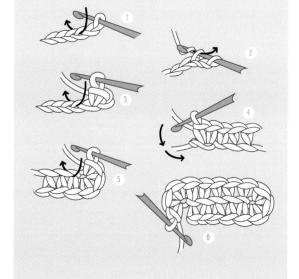

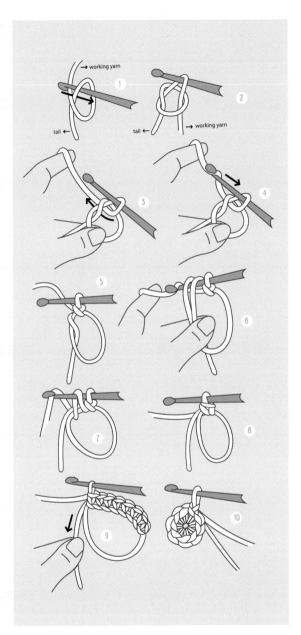

MAGIC RING

To start an amigurumi piece, you often need a little circle. A magic ring is the ideal way to start crocheting in the round as there will be no hole left in the middle of your starting round. You start by crocheting over an adjustable loop and finally pull the loop tight when you have finished the required number of stitches.

Step 1: Start with the yarn crossed to form a circle.

Step 2: Draw up a loop with your hook, but don't pull it tight.

Step 3: Hold the circle with your index finger and thumb and wrap the working yarn over your middle finger.

Step 4-5: Make one chain stitch by wrapping the yarn over the hook and pulling it through the loop on the hook.

Step 6: Now insert your hook into the circle and underneath the tail. Wrap the yarn over the hook and draw up a loop.

Step 7: Keep your hook above the circle and wrap the yarn over the hook again.

Step 8: Pull it through both loops on the hook. You have now completed your first single crochet stitch.

Continue to crochet (repeating step 6, 7, 8) until you have the required number of stitches as mentioned in the pattern.

Step 9-10: Now grab the yarn tail and pull to draw the center of the ring tightly.

You can now begin your second round by crocheting into the first single crochet stitch of the magic ring. You can use a stitch marker to remember where you started.

Challenging? You can try the alternative method. Tutorial on the next page →

Scan or visit
www.stitch.show/
magicring
for the video tutorial

↓

STARTING A CIRCULAR PIECE WITH 2 CHAIN STITCHES

If you don't want to use the magic ring technique, there's an easier way to start crocheting in the round. The downside of this technique is a tiny hole that remains visible in the center of the piece.

Step 1: Start by making a slip knot. Then, make 2 chain stitches and work x sc into the second chain from the hook — where x is the number of sc stitches you would make in your magic ring.

Step 2: Make a slst in the first stitch. You now have a little circle to start with.

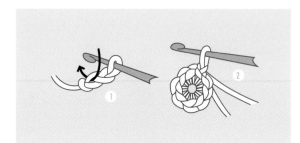

CROCHET INTO A RING

Step 1: When you want a center ring that is open, you start with a series of chain stitches and close with a slip stitch in the first chain to make a ring.

Step 2: Insert your hook into the center of the ring, instead of into the chain stitch and complete the stitch in the usual way. Follow the pattern instructions to determine how many stitches to work into the ring.

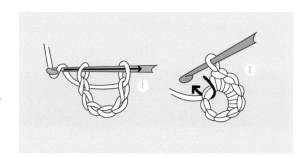

CROCHET IN THE BACK RIDGE OF A CHAIN

Usually you crochet in the front side of the chain, which looks like a series of interlocking V's.

Step 1: Turn your chain.

Step 2: You'll see a small 'hump' on the back side of each stitch (marked in blue). Insert your hook under this hump and continue as usual.

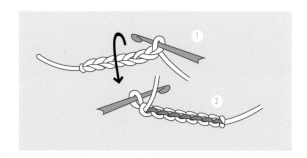

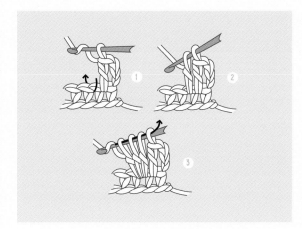

BOBBLE STITCH (abbreviation: 3-dc-bobble)

The bobble stitch creates a soft dimensional bobble. Think of it as a cluster of dc stitches worked in the same stitch.

Step 1: Bring your yarn over the hook from back to front before placing the hook in the stitch.

Step 2: Wrap the yarn over the hook and draw the yarn through the stitch. You now have three loops on the hook. Wrap the yarn over the hook again and pull it through the first two loops on the hook. One half-closed double crochet is complete, and two loops remain on the hook.

Step 3: In the same stitch, repeat the preceding steps twice. You should have four loops on your hook. Wrap the yarn over your hook and draw the yarn through all loops on the hook. You have now completed one 3-dc-bobble stitch. Create a bobble stitch with as many dc stitches as indicated in the pattern.

Scan or visit
www.stitch.show/ bobble for the video tutorial

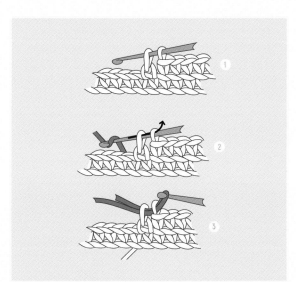

COLOR CHANGE – INVISIBLE COLOR CHANGE

When you want to switch from one color to the next, you work to within two stitches before a color change.

Step 1: Make the next single crochet stitch as usual, but don't pull the final loop through.

Step 2-3: Instead, wrap the new color of yarn around your hook and pull it through the remaining loops.

To make a neat color change, you can make the first stitch in the new color a slip stitch instead of a single crochet. Don't pull the slip stitch too tight or it will be difficult to crochet into in the next round. Tie the loose tails in a knot and leave them on the inside.

Scan or visit
www.stitch.show/ colorchange for the video tutorial

COLOR CHANGE – JACQUARD

When working jacquard, you work with two colors and leave the yarn you don't use on the back (inside) of the work. When it's time to use it again, you pick up the yarn and carry it across the back (inside) of your work before making the next color change. Take into account that a color change always starts a stitch before. The strands that remain inside your crochetwork between color changes must be loose enough so that the fabric doesn't pucker.

Scan or visit **www.stitch.show/ jacquard** for the video tutorial

FASTENING OFF

Step 1: When you've finished crocheting, cut the yarn a couple of inches / cm from your last stitch. Pull the yarn through the last loop until it is all the way through. You now have a finished knot.

Step 2: Thread the long tail through a tapestry needle and insert it through the back loop of the next stitch. This way the finishing knot will remain invisible in your finished piece. You can use this yarn tail to continue sewing the pieces together.

Scan or visit **www.stitch.show/ fastenoff** for the video tutorial

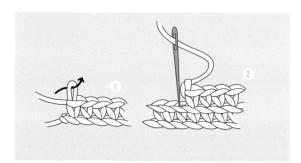

CLOSING OFF A PIECE

Step 1: After several decreases in the last round, a small hole will remain at the end of some pieces.

Step 2: Fasten off, leaving a long yarn tail. Thread the yarn tail left at the end of the piece onto a yarn needle, then insert the needle through each of the front loops of the stitches in the last round. Tighten and insert the needle through the nearest stitch, make a knot, and hide the yarn tail inside the piece.

Scan or visit **www.stitch.show/ closing** for the video tutorial

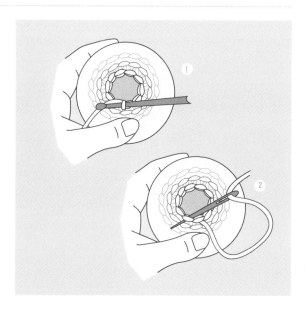

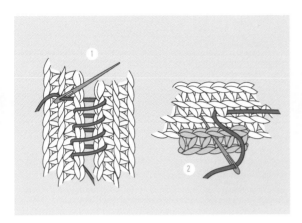

TIP: Always make sure the pieces are securely attached so that they can't be pulled off. Make small, neat stitches and try to make them show as little as possible.

JOINING PARTS – SEWING

First, pin the parts you want to sew to one another, so you can evaluate the result and adjust if necessary. If possible, use the leftover yarn tail from when you fastened off, or use a new length of the same yarn color of one of the pieces that you want to join.

Option 1 – When the different pieces are open: position the piece on the body and sew all around it, going through the stitches of both the extremity and the body.

Option 2 – When the opening of the different pieces is sewn closed before attaching them to the body: line up the stitches and sew through both loops of the open side and between the stitches of the closed side. Use the same color of yarn as the pieces you want to join together.

Scan or visit
**www.stitch.show/
joining-sewing**
for the video tutorial

EMBELLISHMENT – SURFACE SLIP STITCH

The surface slip stitch is an embellishment of slip stitches worked on top of the fabric of your crochetwork.

Step 1: Insert the hook from the right side to the wrong side where you want your line of slip stitches to start, now wrap the yarn over the hook and draw it through the stitch.

Step 2: Insert the hook in the next stitch, wrap the yarn over the hook. Pull it through the stitch and the loop on the hook. This is the start of your line of surface slip stitches.

Step 3: Repeat this to the end of your crochetwork or in any shape you like.

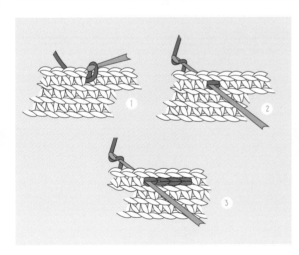

Scan or visit
**www.stitch.show/
surfaceslst**
for the video tutorial

EMBELLISHMENT – FRENCH KNOT

Step 1: Insert the tapestry needle from the back to the front through the stitch where you want the knot to show. Keep the tip of the needle flat against your crochetwork and wrap the yarn around your needle twice.

Step 2: Carefully pull the needle through these loops so that you end up with a double knot. Insert the needle in the crochet stitch next to the knot – not in the same stitch, as this will make the knot disappear – and fasten at the back.

Scan or visit
**www.stitch.show/
frenchknot**
for the video tutorial

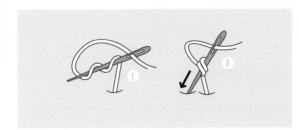

Hector
THE CYCLOPS

A DESIGN BY DIY FLUFFIES (MARISKA VOS-BOLMAN)

Hector the Cyclops lives in a small village at the base of a mountain. Despite his large size and strength, Hector is notoriously lazy. He spends his days lounging in the sun, dozing off, and coming up with elaborate excuses for not helping with the village chores.

Skill level: ★(★)
Size: 8.5 in / 22 cm tall when made with the indicated yarn

Amigurumi gallery: Scan or visit www.amigurumi.com/4401 to share pictures and find inspiration.

YOU WILL NEED:
Worsted weight furry yarn
● brown (3 balls)
Sport weight yarn
● beige
white
● green (leftover)
● black (leftover)
H-8 / 5 mm and B-1 / 2.5 mm crochet hooks
Scissors
Yarn needle
Pins
Fiberfill

Note: The designer used Schachenmayr Brazilia for Hector's body, an eyelash yarn, but any furry yarn alternative will give a cute look.
Note: Use a B-1 / 2.5 mm crochet hook, unless the pattern states otherwise.

BODY (in brown furry yarn, with a H-8 / 5 mm crochet hook)
Rnd 1: start 6 sc in a magic ring [6]
Rnd 2: inc in all 6 st [12]
Rnd 3: (sc in next st, inc in next st) repeat 6 times [18]
Rnd 4: (sc in next 2 st, inc in next st) repeat 6 times [24]
Rnd 5: (sc in next 3 st, inc in next st) repeat 6 times [30]
Rnd 6: (sc in next 4 st, inc in next st) repeat 6 times [36]
Rnd 7: (sc in next 5 st, inc in next st) repeat 6 times [42]
Rnd 8: (sc in next 6 st, inc in next st) repeat 6 times [48]
Rnd 9: (sc in next 7 st, inc in next st) repeat 6 times [54]
Rnd 10: (sc in next 8 st, inc in next st) repeat 6 times [60]
Rnd 11 – 16: sc in all 60 st [60]
Mark a stitch of round 12 with a stitch marker. This will help you to position the horn later.
Rnd 17: (sc in next 9 st, inc in next st) repeat 6 times [66]
Rnd 18 – 28: sc in all 66 st [66]

Mark a stitch of round 18 with a stitch marker. This will help you to position the eyes later.
Rnd 29: (sc in next 10 st, inc in next st) repeat 6 times [72]
Rnd 30 – 48: sc in all 72 st [72]
Rnd 49: (sc in next 10 st, dec) repeat 6 times [66]
Rnd 50: (sc in next 9 st, dec) repeat 6 times [60]
Rnd 51: (sc in next 8 st, dec) repeat 6 times [54]
Rnd 52: (sc in next 7 st, dec) repeat 6 times [48]
Rnd 53: (sc in next 4 st, dec) repeat 8 times [40]
Stuff the body with fiberfill and continue stuffing as you go.
Rnd 54: (sc in next 3 st, dec) repeat 8 times [32]
Rnd 55: (sc in next 2 st, dec) repeat 8 times [24]
Rnd 56: (sc in next st, dec) repeat 8 times [16]
Rnd 57: dec 8 times [8]
Fasten off, leaving a long yarn tail. Using your yarn needle, weave the yarn tail through the front loop

of each remaining stitch and pull it tight to close. Weave in the yarn end.

EYE (start in black yarn)

Rnd 1: start 6 sc in a magic ring [6]

Rnd 2: inc in all 6 st [12]

Change to green yarn.

Rnd 3: (sc in next st, inc in next st) repeat 6 times [18]

Rnd 4: (sc in next 2 st, inc in next st) repeat 6 times [24]

Rnd 5: (sc in next 3 st, inc in next st) repeat 6 times [30]

Change to white yarn.

Rnd 6: (sc in next 4 st, inc in next st) repeat 6 times [36]

Rnd 7: (sc in next 5 st, inc in next st) repeat 6 times [42]

Rnd 8: sc in all 42 st [42]

Rnd 9: (sc in next 6 st, inc in next st) repeat 6 times [48]

Rnd 10 – 11: sc in all 48 st [48]

Fasten off, leaving a long tail for sewing. Stuff the eye with fiberfill. Sew it between rounds 18 and 31 of the body.

EYELID (in beige yarn)

Crochet in rows.

Row 1: start 3 sc in a magic ring, ch 1, turn [3]

Row 2: inc in all 3 st, ch 1, turn [6]

Row 3: (sc in next st, inc in next st) repeat 3 times, ch 1, turn [9]

Row 4: (sc in next 2 st, inc in next st) repeat 3 times, ch 1, turn [12]

Row 5: (sc in next 3 st, inc in next st) repeat 3 times, ch 1, turn [15]

Row 6: (sc in next 4 st, inc in next st) repeat 3 times, ch 1, turn [18]

Row 7: (sc in next 5 st, inc in next st) repeat 3 times, ch 1, turn [21]

Row 8: sc in all 21 st, ch 1, turn [21]

Row 9: (sc in next 6 st, inc in next st) repeat 3 times, ch 1, turn [24]

Row 10: sc in all 24 st, ch 1, turn [24]

Row 11: sc in all 24 st [24]

Fasten off, leaving a long tail for sewing. Sew the eyelid over the top side of the eye, so that it covers almost half of the eye.

HORN (make 2, in white yarn)

Rnd 1: start 4 sc in a magic ring [4]

Rnd 2: inc in all 4 st [8]

Rnd 3: sc in all 8 st [8]

Rnd 4: (sc in next st, inc in next st) repeat 4 times [12]

Rnd 5: sc in all 12 st [12]

Rnd 6: (sc in next 2 st, inc in next st) repeat 4 times [16]

Rnd 7: sc in all 16 st [16]

Rnd 8: (sc in next 3 st, inc in next st) repeat 4 times [20]

Rnd 9: sc in all 20 st [20]
Rnd 10: (sc in next 4 st, inc in next st) repeat 4 times [24]
Rnd 11: sc in all 24 st [24]
Rnd 12: (sc in next 3 st, inc in next st) repeat 6 times [30]
Rnd 13: sc in all 30 st [30]
Rnd 14: (sc in next 4 st, inc in next st) repeat 6 times [36]
Rnd 15: sc in all 36 st [36]
Fasten off, leaving a long tail for sewing. Stuff the horns with fiberfill. Sew them between rounds 12 and 21 of the body.

ARM (make 2, in beige yarn)
Rnd 1: start 6 sc in a magic ring [6]
Rnd 2: inc in all 6 st [12]
Rnd 3: (sc in next st, inc in next 3 st, sc in next 2 st) repeat 2 times [18]
Rnd 4: sc in next st, (sc in next st, inc in next st) repeat 3 times, sc in next 3 st, (sc in next st, inc in next st) repeat 3 times, sc in next 2 st [24]
Rnd 5 – 9: sc in all 24 st [24]
Stuff the arm with fiberfill and continue stuffing as you go.
Rnd 10: (sc in next 4 st, dec) repeat 4 times [20]
Rnd 11: (sc in next 3 st, dec) repeat 4 times [16]
Rnd 12 – 19: sc in all 16 st [16]
Rnd 20: (sc in next 2 st, dec) repeat 4 times [12]
Rnd 21: dec 6 times [6]
Fasten off, leaving a long yarn tail. Using your yarn needle, weave the yarn tail through the front loop of each remaining stitch and pull it tight to close. Leave a long tail for sewing.

THUMB (make 2, in beige yarn)
Rnd 1: start 5 sc in a magic ring [5]
Rnd 2: inc in all 5 st [10]
Rnd 3 – 5: sc in all 10 st [10]
Slst in next st. Fasten off, leaving a long tail for sewing.

FINGER (make 6, in beige yarn)
Rnd 1: start 4 sc in a magic ring [4]
Rnd 2: inc in all 4 st [8]
Rnd 3 – 5: sc in all 8 st [8]
Slst in next st. Fasten off, leaving a long tail for sewing. Stuff the thumbs and fingers lightly with fiberfill. Sew the thumb between rounds 5 and 9 of the arm. Sew one finger next to the thumb, with an interspace of 2 stitches. Sew 2 more fingers next to the first finger, without leaving any spaces. Make sure to mirror the left and right arm. Sew the arms to the body at 8 rounds below the horns.

FOOT (make 2, in beige yarn)
Rnd 1: start 6 sc in a magic ring [6]
Rnd 2: inc in all 6 st [12]
Rnd 3: (sc in next st, inc in next 3 st, sc in next 2 st) repeat 2 times [18]
Rnd 4: sc in next st, (sc in next st, inc in next st) repeat 3 times, sc in next 3 st, (sc in next st, inc in next st) repeat 3 times, sc in next 2 st [24]
Rnd 5: sc in next st, (sc in next 2 st, inc in next st) repeat 3 times, sc in next 3 st, (sc in next 2 st, inc in next st) repeat 3 times, sc in next 2 st [30]
Rnd 6 – 10: sc in all 30 st [30]
Rnd 11: (sc in next 3 st, dec) repeat 6 times [24]
Rnd 12 – 17: sc in all 24 st [24]
Stuff the feet with fiberfill and continue stuffing as you go.
Rnd 18: (sc in next 2 st, dec) repeat 6 times [18]
Rnd 19: (sc in next st, dec) repeat 6 times [12]
Rnd 20: dec 6 times [6]
Fasten off, leaving a long yarn tail. Using your yarn needle, weave the yarn tail through the front loop of each remaining stitch and pull it tight to close. Weave in the yarn end.

BIG TOE (make 2, in beige yarn)
Rnd 1: start 6 sc in a magic ring [6]
Rnd 2: inc in all 6 st [12]
Rnd 3 – 5: sc in all 12 st [12]
Rnd 6: (sc in next 2 st, dec) repeat 3 times [9]
Rnd 7: sc in all 9 st [9]
Slst in next st. Fasten off, leaving a long tail for sewing.

SMALL TOE (make 6, in beige yarn)
Rnd 1: start 5 sc in a magic ring [5]
Rnd 2: inc in all 5 st [10]
Rnd 3 – 5: sc in all 10 st [10]
Slst in next st. Fasten off, leaving a long tail for sewing. Stuff the big and small toes lightly with fiberfill. Sew the big toe on the side of the foot, between rounds 2 and 6. Sew the small toes next to the big toe, without leaving any spaces. Make sure to mirror the left and right foot.

LEG (make 2, in beige yarn)
Rnd 1: start 6 sc in a magic ring [6]
Rnd 2: inc in all 6 st [12]
Rnd 3: (sc in next st, inc in next st) repeat 6 times [18]
Rnd 4 – 14: sc in all 18 st [18]
Slst in next st. Fasten off, leaving a long tail for sewing. Stuff the leg with fiberfill and sew the open side to rounds 13-18 of the foot. Sew the legs to the bottom of the body.

Akiko

THE UNICORN

A DESIGN BY ANAVICKY ESPIÑEIRA

A bright little unicorn, Akiko was born under a lucky star and she loves all things related to space. Whether it's stargazing, studying her astronomy books or devising her own rocket project, Akiko can get lost in her imagination and work for hours. She often wishes she could go up in space herself (and those wishes are magical too, as every unicorn wish conjures up a rainbow somewhere else).

Skill level: ★ ★ ★
Size: 12 in / 30 cm tall when
made with the indicated yarn

Amigurumi gallery: Scan or visit
www.amigurumi.com/4402
to share pictures and find inspiration.

YOU WILL NEED:
Light worsted weight yarn
    light pink (2 balls)
    pink (2 balls)
    aqua
    lilac
    purple
    light yellow
    white
    black (leftover)
    green (leftover)
Size C-2 / 2.75 mm crochet hook
Safety eyes (14 mm)
Pink sewing thread
Lilac embroidery thread
Plastic beads
Sewing needle
Yarn needle
Pins
Stitch markers
Fiberfill
Optional: small safety pin (to position the butterfly)

Note: Leave out the plastic beads if you're making the unicorn for children aged 3 and younger.

HEAD (start in pink yarn)
Rnd 1: start 8 sc in a magic ring [8]
Rnd 2: (inc in next st, sc in next 2 st, inc in next st) repeat 2 times [12]
Rnd 3: (inc in next 2 st, sc in next 2 st, inc in next 2 st) repeat 2 times [20]
Rnd 4: (inc in next 2 st, sc in next 6 st, inc in next 2 st) repeat 2 times [28]
Rnd 5: (sc in next st, inc in next st) repeat 2 times, sc in next 6 st, (inc in next st, sc in next st) repeat 2 times, (inc in next st, sc in next st) repeat 2 times, sc in next 6 st, (inc in next st, sc in next st) repeat 2 times [36]

Rnd 6: (sc in next 5 st, inc in next st) repeat 6 times [42]
Rnd 7 – 9: sc in all 42 st [42]
Rnd 10: (sc in next 3 st, inc in next st, sc in next 3 st) repeat 6 times [48]
Rnd 11 – 12: sc in all 48 st [48]
Sc in next 12 st and mark the last stitch with a stitch marker. This is the new end of your round. Change to light pink yarn.
Rnd 13: sc in all 48 st [48]
Rnd 14: sc in next 12 st, (inc in next st, sc in next st) repeat 6 times, (sc in next st, inc in next st) repeat 6 times, sc in next 12 st [60]
Rnd 15: sc in all 60 st [60]
Rnd 16: sc in next 12 st, (inc in next st, sc in next 2 st) repeat 6 times, (sc in next 2 st, inc in next st) repeat 6 times, sc in next 12 st [72]
Rnd 17 – 20: sc in all 72 st [72]
Rnd 21: (sc in next 11 st, inc in next st) repeat 6 times [78]
Rnd 22 – 31: sc in all 78 st [78]
Insert the safety eyes between rounds 17 and 18, with an interspace of 15 stitches (picture 1). Embroider small eyelashes with a strand of black yarn (picture 2) and eye whites below the eyes with a strand of white yarn.
Rnd 32: (sc in next 11 st, dec) repeat 6 times [72]
Rnd 33 – 34: sc in all 72 st [72]
Rnd 35: (sc in next 5 st, dec, sc in next 5 st) repeat 6 times [66]
Rnd 36: sc in all 66 st [66]
Rnd 37: (sc in next 9 st, dec) repeat 6 times [60]
Rnd 38: (sc in next 4 st, dec, sc in next 4 st) repeat 6 times [54]
Rnd 39: (sc in next 7 st, dec) repeat 6 times [48]
Rnd 40: (sc in next 3 st, dec, sc in next 3 st) repeat 6 times [42]
Rnd 41: (sc in next 5 st, dec) repeat 6 times [36]
Stuff the head with fiberfill and continue stuffing as you go.

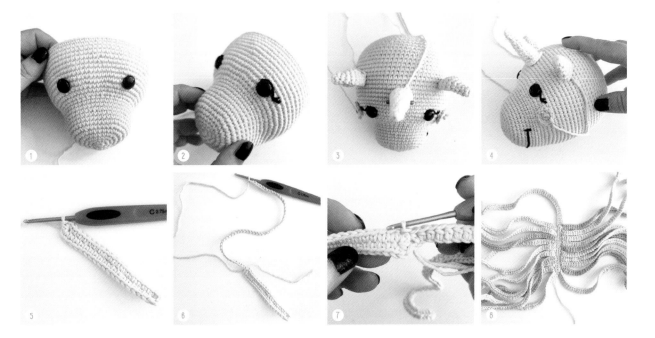

Rnd 42: (sc in next 4 st, dec) repeat 6 times [30]
Rnd 43: (sc in next 3 st, dec) repeat 6 times [24]
Rnd 44: (sc in next 2 st, dec) repeat 6 times [18]
Rnd 45: (sc in next st, dec) repeat 6 times [12]
Rnd 46: dec 6 times [6]
Fasten off, leaving a long yarn tail. Using your yarn needle, weave the yarn tail through the front loop of each remaining stitch and pull it tight to close. Weave in the yarn end. Embroider a big smile on round 10 of the head with a strand of black yarn.

EAR (make 2, in light pink yarn)
Rnd 1: start 5 sc in a magic ring [5]
Rnd 2: sc in all 5 st [5]
Rnd 3: inc in all 5 st [10]
Rnd 4: (sc in next st, inc in next st) repeat 5 times [15]
Rnd 5: (sc in next 2 st, inc in next st) repeat 5 times [20]
Rnd 6: sc in all 20 st [20]
Rnd 7: (sc in next 2 st, dec) repeat 5 times [15]

Rnd 8: (sc in next st, dec) repeat 5 times [10]
Rnd 9: sc in all 10 st [10]
Slst in next st. Fasten off, leaving a long tail for sewing. The ears don't need to be stuffed. Flatten the ears and sew them to the head at about 7 rounds above the eyes, with an interspace of approx. 18 stitches.

HORN (in white yarn)
Rnd 1: start 4 sc in a magic ring [4]
Rnd 2: inc in next st, sc in next 3 st [5]
Rnd 3: sc in next 2 st, inc in next st, sc in next 2 st [6]
Rnd 4: inc in next st, sc in next 5 st [7]
Rnd 5: sc in next 3 st, inc in next st, sc in next 3 st [8]
Rnd 6: inc in next st, sc in next 7 st [9]
Rnd 7: sc in next 4 st, inc in next st, sc in next 4 st [10]
Rnd 8: inc in next st, sc in next 9 st [11]
Rnd 9: sc in next 5 st, inc in next st, sc in next 5 st [12]
Rnd 10: inc in next st, sc in next 11 st [13]
Rnd 11 – 12: sc in all 13 st [13]

Slst in next st. Fasten off, leaving a long tail for sewing. Stuff the horn with fiberfill. Pin the horn between rounds 20 and 23 of the head and sew it on (picture 3).

CHEEK (make 2, in pink yarn)
Rnd 1: start 5 sc in a magic ring [5]
Rnd 2: inc in all 5 st [10]
Slst in next st. Fasten off, leaving a long tail for sewing. Sew the cheeks underneath the eyes (picture 4).

MANE (start in light pink yarn)
To make the mane, we start with an oval piece, adding strands in different colors.
Ch 19. Stitches are worked around both sides of the foundation chain.
Rnd 1: start in second ch from hook, inc in this st, sc in next 16 st, 5 sc in next st. Continue on the other side of the foundation chain, sc in next 16 st, 3 sc in next st [42] (picture 5)
In the next round, we'll make 21 strands. Change to aqua yarn.
Rnd 2: (ch 52 (picture 6), start in third ch from hook, 2 hdc in next 15 ch, hdc in next 35 ch, skip 1 st and slst in next st of round 1) (picture 7),
change to purple yarn and repeat the pattern,
change to pink yarn and repeat the pattern,
change to lilac yarn and repeat the pattern,
continue alternating the pattern in aqua, purple,

pink and lilac yarn until you've reached the end [21 strands] (picture 8)
Slst in next st. Fasten off, leaving a long tail for sewing. Pin round 1 of the mane to the head, just behind the horn. Sew the mane to the head (picture 9). To finish, flip all the strands to one side of the head and style the mane as you like (picture 10).

BODY: NECK AND BACK (in light pink yarn)
Leave a long starting yarn tail. Ch 24 and join with a slst to make a circle.
Rnd 1 – 3: sc in all 24 st [24]
Rnd 4: sc in next 6 st, inc in next st, sc in next 10 st, inc in next st, sc in next 6 st [26]
Rnd 5 – 6: sc in all 26 st [26]
Rnd 7: sc in next 7 st, inc in next st, sc in next 10 st, inc in next st, sc in next 7 st [28]
Rnd 8: sc in all 28 st [28]
In the next round, we start making the back.
Rnd 9: ch 15 (picture 11), start in second ch from hook, inc in this ch, sc in next 13 ch (picture 12), sc in next 28 st of the neck. Continue on the other side of the foundation chain, sc in next 13 ch, inc in last ch [58] (picture 13)
Rnd 10: inc in next 2 st, sc in next 54 st, inc in next 2 st [62]
Rnd 11: (sc in next st, inc in next st) repeat 2 times, sc in next 54 st, (inc in next st, sc in next st) repeat 2 times [66]
Rnd 12: (sc in next 2 st, inc in next st) repeat 2 times, sc in next 54 st, (inc in next st, sc in next 2 st) repeat

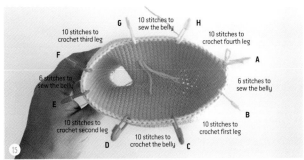

G — 10 stitches to sew the belly — H
10 stitches to crochet third leg
F
10 stitches to crochet fourth leg
A
6 stitches to sew the belly
E
6 stitches to sew the belly
B
10 stitches to crochet second leg
D
10 stitches to crochet the belly
C
10 stitches to crochet first leg

2 times [70]

Rnd 13: (sc in next 3 st, inc in next st) repeat 2 times, sc in next 54 st, (inc in next st, sc in next 3 st) repeat 2 times [74]

Rnd 14: (sc in next 4 st, inc in next st) repeat 2 times, sc in next 54 st, (inc in next st, sc in next 4 st) repeat 2 times [78]

Rnd 15 – 28: sc in all 78 st [78]

Rnd 29: (sc in next 11 st, dec) repeat 6 times [72] (picture 14)

Fasten off and weave in the yarn end. Mark the last stitch of round 29 with a stitch marker.

To continue making the legs and the belly, turn the body upside down and mark 8 sections with stitch markers (picture 15). Start counting from the marked stitch of round 29, this is marker A.

• count 6 st to the left and place marker B (6 stitches to sew the belly)
• count 10 st to the left and place marker C (10 stitches for the first leg)
• count 10 st to the left and place marker D (10 stitches for the belly)
• count 10 st to the left and place marker E (10 stitches for the second leg)
• count 6 st to the left and place marker F (6 stitches to sew the belly)
• count 10 st to the left and place marker G (10 stitches for the third leg)

- count 10 st to the left and place marker H (10 stitches to sew the belly).
- the remaining 10 st between H and A are for the fourth leg.

BODY: LEG (make 4, start in light pink yarn)
Pull up a loop of light pink yarn in the first stitch between markers B and C (picture 16). This is where we start the first leg.
Rnd 1: sc in next 10 st, ch 10 [10 + 10 ch] (picture 17) Make sure the chain isn't twisted.
Rnd 2: sc in first st of round 1 to make a circle (picture 18), sc in next 9 st, sc in all 10 ch [20]
Rnd 3 — 4: sc in all 20 st [20]
Rnd 5: (sc in next 9 st, inc in next st) repeat 2 times [22]
Rnd 6 — 8: sc in all 22 st [22]
Rnd 9: (sc in next 10 st, inc in next st) repeat 2 times [24]
Rnd 10 — 12: sc in all 24 st [24]
Rnd 13: (sc in next 11 st, inc in next st) repeat 2 times [26]
Rnd 14 — 16: sc in all 26 st [26]
Rnd 17: (sc in next 12 st, inc in next st) repeat 2 times [28]
Rnd 18 — 20: sc in all 28 st [28]
Rnd 21: (sc in next 13 st, inc in next st) repeat 2 times [30]
Rnd 22 — 24: sc in all 30 st [30]
Change to pink yarn. Stuff the leg firmly with fiberfill and continue stuffing as you go.
Rnd 25: BLO sc in all 30 st [30]
Rnd 26 — 29: sc in all 30 st [30] (picture 19)

Rnd 30: BLO (sc in next 3 st, dec) repeat 6 times [24]

Rnd 31: (sc in next 2 st, dec) repeat 6 times [18]

Rnd 32: (sc in next st, dec) repeat 6 times [12]

Rnd 33: dec 6 times [6]

Fasten off, leaving a long yarn tail. Using your yarn needle, weave the yarn tail through the front loop of each remaining stitch and pull it tight to close. Weave in the yarn end.

Repeat the pattern for the leg 3 more times, between markers D and E (second leg), between markers F and G (third leg) and between markers H and A (fourth leg) (picture 20).

BODY: BELLY (in light pink yarn)

Remove marker C and pull up a loop of light pink yarn in this stitch (picture 21). You'll work up to marker D. Crochet in rows.

Row 1 – 2: sc in all 10 st, ch 1, turn [10]

Row 3: sc in all 10 st, ch 11, turn [10 + 11 ch]

Row 4: start in second ch from hook, sc in all 10 ch, sc in all 10 st, ch 11, turn [20 + 11 ch]

Row 5: start in second ch from hook, sc in all 10 ch, sc in all 20 st, ch 1, turn [30]

Row 6 – 8: sc in all 30 st, ch 1, turn [30]

Row 9: sc in next 20 st, ch 1, turn [20] Leave the remaining stitches unworked.

Row 10: sc in next 10 st, ch 1, turn [10] Leave the remaining stitches unworked.

Row 11: sc in all 10 st, ch 1, turn [10]

Row 12: sc in all 10 st [10]

Fasten off, leaving a very long tail for sewing.

ASSEMBLY OF THE UNICORN BODY

The belly looks a bit like a puzzle piece that closes the unicorn's body (picture 22). Start by sewing the 10 stitches of the last row of the belly to the 10 stitches between markers G and H (picture 23) (you can now remove them). Don't cut the yarn yet. Start stuffing the

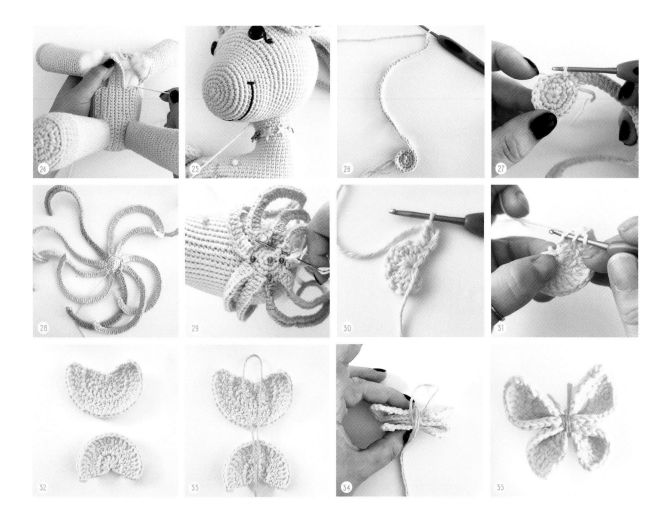

body with fiberfill and continue stuffing as you go -
removing the markers along the way (picture 24).
Continue by sewing the belly to the inside of the legs.
Sew the belly to the 6 stitches left at the front and the
back of the body.

Embroider stars on the body with lilac embroidery
thread and sew colored beads on the body with pink
sewing thread. Pin the head to the neck (picture 25). Tilt
it backward to give your unicorn a cuter look. Sew it on.
Add more fiberfill to the neck before closing the seam.

TAIL (start in light pink yarn)

To make the tail, we start with a circle, adding strands in
different colors.

Rnd 1: start 6 sc in a magic ring [6]

Rnd 2: inc in all 6 st [12]

Rnd 3: (sc in next st, inc in next st) repeat 6 times [18]

In the next round, we'll make 9 strands. Change to
aqua yarn.

Rnd 4: [ch 42 (picture 26), start in third ch from hook,
(2 hdc in next ch, hdc in next ch) repeat 20 times,
skip 1 st on Rnd 3, slst in next st of Rnd 3] (picture 27),

change to purple yarn and repeat the pattern, change to pink yarn and repeat the pattern, change to lilac yarn and repeat the pattern, continue alternating the pattern in aqua, purple, pink and lilac yarn until you've reached the end [9 strands] (picture 28)

Slst in next st. Fasten off, leaving a long tail for sewing. Pin round 3 of the tail to rounds 10-14 on the back of your unicorn. Sew the tail to the body (picture 29).

BUTTERFLY (in light yellow yarn)
To make the butterfly, we make 2 semicircles (a big and a small one) and join them together with a piece of green yarn to shape the wings.

Big semicircle (in light yellow yarn)
Crochet in rows.
Row 1: start ch 2 + 8 dc in a magic ring. Pull the yarn tight to close the semicircle, turn [8]
Row 2: ch 2, dc in same st (picture 30), dc inc in next 7 st, dc in ch-2-space of row 1 (picture 31), turn [16]
Row 3: ch 2, dc inc in next st, (dc in next st, dc inc in next st) repeat 7 times, dc in ch-2-space of row 2, turn [24]
Row 4: ch 2, hdc in next st, hdc inc in next st, (hdc in next 2 st, hdc inc in next st) repeat 7 times, hdc in ch-2-space of row 3 [32]
Fasten off and weave in the yarn end.

Small semicircle (in light yellow yarn)
Crochet in rows.
Row 1 – 3: repeat rows 1-3 of the big semicircle.
Fasten off and weave in the yarn end.

ASSEMBLY OF THE BUTTERFLY
Put both semicircles with the curved sides toward each other (picture 32) and fold them together in half (pictures 33-34). Wrap a piece of green yarn around the middle of both semicircles and pull it tight. Make a tight knot and cut the yarn, leaving a 0.4 in / 1 cm yarn tail for the butterfly antennae (picture 35). You can attach the butterfly to the unicorn with a safety pin so that it's removable, or sew it on.

Elio

THE DRAGON

A DESIGN BY DIY FLUFFIES (MARISKA VOS-BOLMAN)

Elio, a fearless dragon of the mountain region, bravely guards the nearby small town from the terrors of the dark forest. In recognition of his bravery and protection, the grateful townspeople reward him with plums and grapes, his beloved fruits, which he happily accepts.

Skill level: ★
Size: 8 in / 20 cm tall when made with the indicated yarn

Amigurumi gallery: Scan or visit www.amigurumi.com/4403 to share pictures and find inspiration.

YOU WILL NEED:

Sport weight yarn
- purple (3 balls)
- green
- light green
- white

B-1 / 2.5 mm crochet hook
Safety eyes (12 mm)
Scissors
Yarn needle
Pins
Fiberfill

HEAD (in purple yarn)

Rnd 1: start 6 sc in a magic ring [6]
Rnd 2: inc in all 6 st [12]
Rnd 3: (sc in next st, inc in next st) repeat 6 times [18]
Rnd 4: (sc in next 2 st, inc in next st) repeat 6 times [24]
Rnd 5: (sc in next 3 st, inc in next st) repeat 6 times [30]
Rnd 6: (sc in next 4 st, inc in next st) repeat 6 times [36]
Rnd 7: (sc in next 5 st, inc in next st) repeat 6 times [42]
Rnd 8: (sc in next 6 st, inc in next st) repeat 6 times [48]
Rnd 9 – 10: sc in all 48 st [48]
Rnd 11: (sc in next 7 st, inc in next st) repeat 6 times [54]
Rnd 12 – 13: sc in all 54 st [54]
Rnd 14: (sc in next 8 st, inc in next st) repeat 6 times [60]
Rnd 15 – 22: sc in all 60 st [60]
Insert the safety eyes between rounds 16 and 17, with an interspace of 9 stitches.
Rnd 23: (sc in next 8 st, dec) repeat 6 times [54]
Rnd 24: sc in all 54 st [54]
Rnd 25: (sc in next 7 st, dec) repeat 6 times [48]
Rnd 26: (sc in next 6 st, dec) repeat 6 times [42]
Rnd 27: (sc in next 5 st, dec) repeat 6 times [36]
Stuff the head with fiberfill and continue stuffing as you go.

Rnd 28: (sc in next 4 st, dec) repeat 6 times [30]
Rnd 29: (sc in next 3 st, dec) repeat 6 times [24]
Rnd 30: (sc in next 2 st, dec) repeat 6 times [18]
Rnd 31: (sc in next st, dec) repeat 6 times [12]
Rnd 32: dec 6 times [6]
Fasten off, leaving a long yarn tail. Using your yarn needle, weave the yarn tail through the front loop of each remaining stitch and pull it tight to close. Weave in the yarn end.

BODY (in purple yarn)

Rnd 1: start 8 sc in a magic ring [8]
Rnd 2: inc in all 8 st [16]
Rnd 3: (sc in next st, inc in next st) repeat 8 times [24]
Rnd 4: (sc in next 2 st, inc in next st) repeat 8 times [32]
Rnd 5: (sc in next 3 st, inc in next st) repeat 8 times [40]
Rnd 6: (sc in next 4 st, inc in next st) repeat 8 times [48]
Rnd 7: sc in all 48 st [48]
Rnd 8: (sc in next 5 st, inc in next st) repeat 8 times [56]
Rnd 9 – 11: sc in all 56 st [56]
Rnd 12: (sc in next 6 st, inc in next st) repeat 8 times [64]
Rnd 13 – 19: sc in all 64 st [64]
Rnd 20: (sc in next 14 st, dec) repeat 4 times [60]
Rnd 21: sc in all 60 st [60]
Rnd 22: (sc in next 8 st, dec) repeat 6 times [54]
Rnd 23: (sc in next 7 st, dec) repeat 6 times [48]
Rnd 24: sc in all 48 st [48]
Rnd 25: (sc in next 6 st, dec) repeat 6 times [42]
Rnd 26: sc in all 42 st [42]
Rnd 27: (sc in next 5 st, dec) repeat 6 times [36]
Rnd 28 – 30: sc in all 36 st [36]
Rnd 31: (sc in next 4 st, dec) repeat 6 times [30]
Rnd 32 – 37: sc in all 30 st [30]
Slst in next st. Fasten off, leaving a long tail for sewing. Stuff the body with fiberfill and sew it between rounds 28 and 29 of the head. Add more fiberfill to the neck before closing the seam.

SNOUT (in purple yarn)
Rnd 1: start 6 sc in a magic ring [6]
Rnd 2: inc in all 6 st [12]
Rnd 3: (sc in next st, inc in next st) repeat 6 times [18]
Rnd 4: (sc in next 2 st, inc in next st) repeat 6 times [24]
Rnd 5: (sc in next 3 st, inc in next st) repeat 6 times [30]
Rnd 6: (sc in next 4 st, inc in next st) repeat 6 times [36]
Rnd 7 – 9: sc in all 36 st [36]
Rnd 10: (sc in next 4 st, dec) repeat 6 times [30]
Slst in next st. Fasten off, leaving a long tail for sewing. Stuff the snout with fiberfill. Sew the snout between rounds 16 and 27 of the head. The top side of the snout should touch the safety eyes.

NOSTRILS (make 2, in purple yarn)
Crochet in rows.
Row 1: start 3 sc in a magic ring, ch 1, turn [3]
Row 2: inc in all 3 st [6] (picture 1)
Fasten off, leaving a long tail for sewing. Slightly bend the nostrils and sew them to round 6 of the snout (picture 2).

EAR (make 2, in purple yarn)
Rnd 1: start 4 sc in a magic ring [4]
Rnd 2: (sc in next st, inc in next st) repeat 2 times [6]
Rnd 3: (sc in next 2 st, inc in next st) repeat 2 times [8]
Rnd 4: (sc in next 3 st, inc in next st) repeat 2 times [10]
Rnd 5: (sc in next 4 st, inc in next st) repeat 2 times [12]

Rnd 6: sc in all 12 st [12]
Slst in next st. Fasten off, leaving a long tail for sewing. Flatten the ears, they don't need to be stuffed. Sew them between rounds 10 and 16 of the head.

BELLY (in light green yarn)
Ch 7. Crochet in rows.
Row 1: start in second ch from hook, sc in next 6 ch, ch 1, turn [6]
Row 2: inc in next st, sc in next 4 st, inc in next st, ch 1, turn [8]
Row 3: inc in next st, sc in next 6 st, inc in next st, ch 1, turn [10]
Row 4 – 5: sc in all 10 st, ch 1, turn [10]
Row 6: inc in next st, sc in next 8 st, inc in next st, ch 1, turn [12]
Row 7: sc in all 12 st, ch 1, turn [12]
Row 8: inc in next st, sc in next 10 st, inc in next st, ch 1, turn [14]
Row 9: sc in all 14 st, ch 1, turn [14]
Row 10: inc in next st, sc in next 12 st, inc in next st, ch 1, turn [16]
Row 11: sc in all 16 st, ch 1, turn [16]
Row 12: inc in next st, sc in next 14 st, inc in next st, ch 1, turn [18]
Row 13: inc in next st, sc in next 16 st, inc in next st, ch 1, turn [20]
Row 14: sc in all 20 st, ch 1, turn [20]

Row 15: inc in next st, sc in next 18 st, inc in next st, ch 1, turn [22]

Row 16 – 18: sc in all 22 st, ch 1, turn [22]

Row 19: inc in next st, sc in next 20 st, inc in next st, ch 1, turn [24]

Row 20 – 25: sc in all 24 st, ch 1, turn [24]

Row 26: dec, sc in next 20 st, dec, ch 1, turn [22]

Row 27: dec, sc in next 18 st, dec, ch 1, turn [20]

Row 28: dec, sc in next 16 st, dec, ch 1, turn [18]

Row 29: dec, sc in next 14 st, dec, ch 1, turn [16]

Row 30: dec, sc in next 12 st, dec, ch 1, turn [14]

Row 31: dec, sc in next 10 st, dec, ch 1, turn [12]

Row 32: dec, sc in next 8 st, dec, ch 1, turn [10]

Row 33: skip first st, dec, sc in next 4 st, dec, slst in next st [7]

Fasten off, leaving a long tail for sewing. Sew the belly between rounds 3 and 36 of the body. Use green yarn to embroider eight horizontal stripes on the belly, with approx. 4 rows between them.

TAIL (in purple yarn)

Rnd 1: start 6 sc in a magic ring [6]

Rnd 2: inc in all 6 st [12]

Rnd 3 – 4: sc in all 12 st [12]

Rnd 5: (sc in next 3 st, inc in next st) repeat 3 times [15]

Rnd 6 – 8: sc in all 15 st [15]

Rnd 9: (sc in next 4 st, inc in next st) repeat 3 times [18]

Rnd 10 – 13: sc in all 18 st [18]

Rnd 14: (sc in next 5 st, inc in next st) repeat 3 times [21]

Rnd 15 – 20: sc in all 21 st [21]

Rnd 21: (sc in next 6 st, inc in next st) repeat 3 times [24]

Rnd 22 – 26: sc in all 24 st [24]

Rnd 27: (sc in next 7 st, inc in next st) repeat 3 times [27]

Rnd 28 – 32: sc in all 27 st [27]

Rnd 33: (sc in next 8 st, inc in next st) repeat 3 times [30]

Rnd 34 – 35: sc in all 30 st [30]

Rnd 36: (sc in next 4 st, inc in next st) repeat 6 times [36]

Rnd 37 – 38: sc in all 36 st [36]

Rnd 39: (sc in next 5 st, inc in next st) repeat 6 times [42]

Rnd 40: sc in all 42 st [42]

Rnd 41: (sc in next 6 st, inc in next st) repeat 6 times [48]

Rnd 42: sc in all 48 st [48]

Slst in next st. Fasten off, leaving a long tail for sewing. Stuff the tail with fiberfill and sew it to the back of the body, between rounds 5 and 23.

HAUNCH (make 2, in purple yarn)

Rnd 1: start 6 sc in a magic ring [6]

Rnd 2: inc in all 6 st [12]

Rnd 3: (sc in next st, inc in next st) repeat 6 times [18]

Rnd 4: (sc in next 2 st, inc in next st) repeat 6 times [24]

Rnd 5: (sc in next 3 st, inc in next st) repeat 6 times [30]

Rnd 6: (sc in next 4 st, inc in next st) repeat 6 times [36]

Rnd 7 – 12: sc in all 36 st [36]

Stuff the haunch lightly with fiberfill and continue stuffing as you go. Be careful not to overstuff.

Rnd 13: (sc in next 4 st, dec) repeat 6 times [30]

Rnd 14: (sc in next 3 st, dec) repeat 6 times [24]

Rnd 15: sc in all 24 st [24]

Rnd 16: (sc in next 2 st, dec) repeat 6 times [18]

Rnd 17: sc in all 18 st [18]

Rnd 18: (sc in next st, dec) repeat 6 times [12]

Rnd 19: dec 6 times [6]

Fasten off, leaving a long yarn tail. Using your yarn needle, weave the yarn tail through the front loop of each remaining stitch and pull it tight to close. Leave a long tail for sewing. Flatten the haunch a bit. Sew the haunches on both sides of the body, between rounds 9 and 21 (pictures 3-4).

LEG (make 2, in purple yarn)
Rnd 1: start 6 sc in a magic ring [6]
Rnd 2: inc in all 6 st [12]
Rnd 3: (sc in next st, inc in next st) repeat 6 times [18]
Rnd 4: (sc in next 2 st, inc in next st) repeat 6 times [24]
Rnd 5 – 8: sc in all 24 st [24]
Stuff the leg lightly with fiberfill and continue stuffing as you go. Be careful not to overstuff.
Rnd 9: (sc in next 2 st, dec) repeat 6 times [18]
Rnd 10: (sc in next st, dec) repeat 6 times [12]
Rnd 11 – 13: sc in all 12 st [12]
Rnd 14: dec 6 times [6]
Fasten off, leaving a long yarn tail. Using your yarn needle, weave the yarn tail through the front loop of each remaining stitch and pull it tight to close. Leave a long tail for sewing.

TOENAIL (make 6, in white yarn)
Rnd 1: start 4 sc in a magic ring [4]
Rnd 2: (sc in next st, inc in next st) repeat 2 times [6]
Slst in next st. Fasten off, leaving a long tail for sewing. Sew one nail over round 1 of the leg. Sew the other two nails on both sides of the first nail, over rounds 4 and 5. Sew the legs to the haunches (picture 5).

ARM (make 2, in purple yarn)
Rnd 1: start 6 sc in a magic ring [6]
Rnd 2: inc in all 6 st [12]
Rnd 3: (sc in next st, inc in next st) repeat 6 times [18]
Rnd 4 – 6: sc in all 18 st [18]
Stuff the arm with fiberfill and continue stuffing as you go.
Rnd 7: (sc in next st, dec) repeat 6 times [12]
Rnd 8 – 13: sc in all 12 st [12]
Rnd 14: dec 6 times [6]

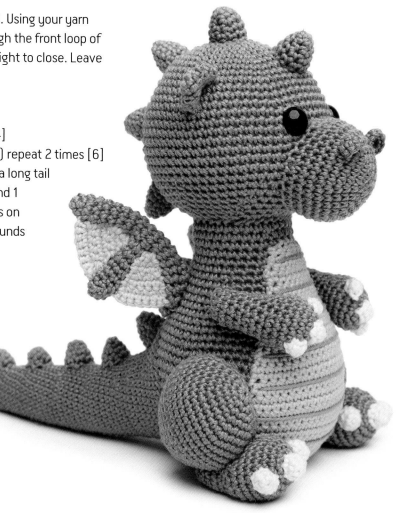

Fasten off, leaving a long yarn tail. Using your yarn needle, weave the yarn tail through the front loop of each remaining stitch and pull it tight to close. Leave a long tail for sewing.

NAIL (make 6, in white yarn)
Rnd 1: start 5 sc in a magic ring [5]
Slst in next st. Fasten off, leaving a long tail for sewing. Sew one nail over round 1 of the arm. Sew the other two nails on both sides of the first nail, over rounds 3 and 4. Sew the arms to the body, between rounds 26 and 29. Sew the inside of the arms to the body and the belly with a few stitches (pictures 6-7).

BIG SPIKE (make 7, in green yarn)
Rnd 1: start 4 sc in a magic ring [4]
Rnd 2: (sc in next st, inc in next st) repeat 2 times [6]
Rnd 3: (sc in next 2 st, inc in next st) repeat 2 times [8]
Rnd 4: (sc in next 3 st, inc in next st) repeat 2 times [10]
Rnd 5: sc in all 10 st [10]
Fasten off, leaving a long tail for sewing. Stuff the spikes lightly with fiberfill. Sew the spikes on the head:
• Sew one spike over rounds 1-2 of the head.
• Sew two spikes over rounds 6-11 of the head (one at the front and one at the back).
• Sew one spike over rounds 14-19, at the back of the head.
• Sew one spike over rounds 22-27, at the back of

the head).
• Sew one spike on the body over rounds 26-32.
• Sew one spike on the tail over rounds 38-42.

MEDIUM SPIKE (make 2, in green yarn)
Rnd 1: start 4 sc in a magic ring [4]
Rnd 2: (sc in next st, inc in next st) repeat 2 times [6]
Rnd 3: (sc in next 2 st, inc in next st) repeat 2 times [8]
Rnd 4: sc in all 8 st [8]
Fasten off, leaving a long tail for sewing. Stuff the spikes lightly with fiberfill. Sew the spikes on the tail:
• Sew one spike over rounds 20-25 of the tail.
• Sew one spike over rounds 28-32 of the tail.

SMALL SPIKE (make 2, in green yarn)
Rnd 1: start 4 sc in a magic ring [4]
Rnd 2: (sc in next st, inc in next st) repeat 2 times [6]
Rnd 3: sc in all 6 st [6]
Fasten off, leaving a long tail for sewing. Stuff the spikes lightly with fiberfill. Sew the spikes to the tip of the tail:
• Sew one spike over rounds 4-9 of the tail.
• Sew one spike over rounds 13-18 of the tail.

WING (make 2)

Wing long branch (in purple yarn)
Rnd 1: start 4 sc in a magic ring [4]
Rnd 2: (sc in next st, inc in next st) repeat 2 times [6]

Row 5 – 6: sc in next 5 st, ch 1, turn [5]
Row 7: inc in next st, sc in next 3 st, inc in next st [7]
Fasten off, leaving a long tail for sewing. Sew the triangular wing webs between the wing branches (pictures 8-9). Sew the wings to the back of the body, between rounds 28-35, with 6 stitches between both wings.

Rnd 3 – 20: sc in all 6 st [6]
Stuff the piece lightly with fiberfill. Fasten off, leaving a long tail for sewing.

Wing short branch (in purple yarn)
Rnd 1: start 4 sc in a magic ring [4]
Rnd 2: (sc in next st, inc in next st) repeat 2 times [6]
Rnd 3 – 8: sc in all 6 st [6]
Stuff the piece lightly with fiberfill. Fasten off, leaving a long tail for sewing. Sew the short branch to round 11 of the long branch.

Wing web (make 2 for each wing, in light green yarn)
Ch 2. Crochet in rows.
Row 1: start in second ch from hook, inc in this ch, ch 1, turn [2]
Row 2: inc in next st, sc in next st, ch 1, turn [3]
Row 3: sc in all 3 st, ch 1, turn [3]
Row 4: inc in next st, sc in next st, inc in next st, ch 1, turn [5]

Alba
THE JACKALOPE

A DESIGN BY LEX IN STITCHES (ALEXA TEMPLETON)

Alba was once just a regular snowshoe hare. During a lightning storm, she suddenly grew her antlers and became a mythical jackalope. Now the Queen of the Forest, Alba gathers flowers for her crown whilst singing sweet songs to all the animals.

Skill level: ★ ★
Size: 8 in / 21 cm tall when
made with the indicated yarn

Amigurumi gallery: Scan or visit
www.amigurumi.com/4404
to share pictures and find inspiration.

YOU WILL NEED:
Fingering weight yarn
- brown
- dark brown (leftover)
- green (leftover)
- pink (leftover)
- yellow (leftover)
- lilac (leftover)

Size B-1 / 2 mm crochet hook
Safety eyes (6 mm)
Black embroidery thread
Sewing needle
Stitch markers
Fiberfill
Optional: pink makeup blush
Optional: small pom pom maker

FOOT (make 2, in brown yarn)
Rnd 1: start 6 sc in a magic ring [6]
Rnd 2: inc in all 6 st [12]
Rnd 3: (inc in next 3 st, sc in next 3 st) repeat 2 times [18]
Rnd 4 – 6: sc in all 18 st [18]
Rnd 7: (sc in next st, dec, sc in next 6 st) repeat 2 times [16]
Rnd 8 – 9: sc in all 16 st [16]
Rnd 10: (sc in next st, dec, sc in next 5 st) repeat 2 times [14]
Rnd 11 – 12: sc in all 14 st [14]
Stuff the foot with fiberfill and continue stuffing as you go.
Rnd 13: (sc in next st, dec, sc in next 4 st) repeat 2 times [12]
Rnd 14: sc in next 3 st, ch 3, skip next 3 st, sc in next 6 st [9 + 3 ch]
Rnd 15: sc in next 3 st, sc in next 3 ch, sc in next 6 st [12]
Rnd 16: sc in all 12 st [12]

Rnd 17: dec 6 times [6]
Fasten off, leaving a yarn tail. Using your yarn needle, weave the yarn tail through the front loop of each remaining stitch and pull it tight to close. Weave in the yarn end. Embroider 2 or 3 straight lines on the foot with a strand of pink yarn.

LEG (make 1 on each foot, in brown yarn)
Pull up a loop of brown yarn in the first skipped stitch on round 14 of the foot. We will be working around this

gap to start the leg.

Rnd 1: sc in next 3 skipped st, sc in the corner space (the space between the skipped st and the ch, marked by a stitch marker in picture 1), sc in next 3 st, sc in the next corner space [8] (picture 1)

Rnd 2: (sc in next st, inc in next st) repeat 4 times [12]

Rnd 3: (sc in next st, inc in next st) repeat 6 times [18]

Fasten off and weave in the yarn end. Stuff the legs firmly with fiberfill. We will join the legs with the belly later to start the body.

BELLY (in brown yarn)

Rnd 1: start 6 sc in a magic ring [6]

Rnd 2: inc in all 6 st [12]

Rnd 3: (sc in next st, inc in next st) repeat 6 times [18]

Rnd 4: (sc in next 2 st, inc in next st) repeat 6 times [24]

Fasten off, leaving a yarn tail.

BODY (in brown yarn)

Start by joining the legs and the belly.

Line up the legs on either side of the belly with both feet pointing forward. Sew 3 stitches on each leg to 3 stitches on the belly (indicated with pink yarn in picture 2, sew with a piece of brown yarn). There should be 18 stitches remaining on the belly after sewing (9 at the front and 9 at the back) and 15 stitches remaining on each leg (48 stitches in total).

Pull up a loop of brown yarn at the back of the belly, at 5 stitches from the left leg (stitch marker in picture 2).

Rnd 1: sc in next 5 st on the back of the belly, sc in next 15 st on the left leg, sc in next 9 st on the front of the belly, sc in next 15 st on the right leg, sc in next 4 st on the back of the belly [48]

Rnd 2: sc in next st, inc in next st, sc in next 2 st, inc in next st, sc in next 16 st, inc in next st, sc in next 2 st, inc in next st, sc in next 2 st, inc in next st, sc in next 17 st, inc in next st, sc in next 2 st [54]

Rnd 3: sc in next 9 st, inc in next st, (sc in next 4 st, inc in next st) repeat 2 times, sc in next 16 st, inc in next st, (sc in next 4 st, inc in next st) repeat 2 times, sc in next 7 st [60]

Rnd 4 – 6: sc in all 60 st [60]

Rnd 7: (sc in next 8 st, dec, sc in next 14 st, dec, sc in next 4 st) repeat 2 times [56]

Rnd 8: sc in all 56 st [56]

Rnd 9: sc in next 8 st, dec, (sc in next 12 st, dec) repeat 3 times, sc in next 4 st [52]

Rnd 10: sc in all 52 st [52]

Rnd 11: (sc in next 8 st, dec, sc in next 10 st, dec, sc in next 4 st) repeat 2 times [48]

Rnd 12: sc in all 48 st [48]

Rnd 13: (sc in next 8 st, dec) repeat 2 times, sc in next 12 st, dec, sc in next 8 st, dec, sc in next 4 st [44]

Rnd 14: sc in all 44 st [44]

Stuff the body with fiberfill and continue stuffing as you go.

Rnd 15: (sc in next 9 st, dec, sc in next 6 st, dec, sc in next 3 st) repeat 2 times [40]

Rnd 16: sc in all 40 st [40]

Rnd 17: (sc in next 2 st, dec) repeat 2 times, sc in next 10 st, dec, (sc in next 2 st, dec) repeat 2 times, sc in next 10 st, dec [34]

Rnd 18: sc in all 34 st [34]

Rnd 19: (sc in next 7 st, dec, sc in next 4 st, dec, sc in next 2 st) repeat 2 times [30]

Rnd 20: sc in all 30 st [30]

Rnd 21: (sc in next 8 st, dec, sc in next 2 st, dec, sc in next st) repeat 2 times [26]

Rnd 22: (sc in next 4 st, dec, sc in next 7 st) repeat 2 times [24]

Rnd 23: sc in all 24 st [24]

Fasten off, leaving a long tail for sewing. Make a small pom pom (approx. 2 in / 5 cm) with brown yarn and sew it to the back of the body.

ARM (make 2, in brown yarn)

Rnd 1: start 6 sc in a magic ring [6]

Rnd 2: (sc in next st, inc in next st) repeat 3 times [9]

Rnd 3 – 18: sc in all 9 st [9]

Stuff the lower half of the arm lightly with fiberfill. Flatten the opening of the arm with the last stitch on the side and work the next round through both layers to close.

Rnd 19: sc in next 4 st [4]

Fasten off, leaving a long tail for sewing. Embroider 2 or 3 straight lines on the arm with a strand of pink yarn. Sew the arms to the sides of the body, slightly slanted over rounds 23-27.

HEAD (in brown yarn)

Rnd 1: start 8 sc in a magic ring [8]

Rnd 2: inc in all 8 st [16]

Rnd 3: (sc in next st, inc in next st) repeat 8 times [24]

Rnd 4: (sc in next 2 st, inc in next st) repeat 8 times [32]

Rnd 5: (sc in next 3 st, inc in next st) repeat 8 times [40]

Rnd 6: sc in next 2 st, inc in next st, (sc in next 4 st, inc in next st) repeat 7 times, sc in next 2 st [48]

Rnd 7: (sc in next 5 st, inc in next st) repeat 8 times [56]

Rnd 8 – 15: sc in all 56 st [56]

Rnd 16: sc in next 12 st, (sc in next st, inc in next st) repeat 6 times, sc in next 4 st *(mark the first and last of these 4 stitches, these mark the position of the*

nose), (inc in next st, sc in next st) repeat 6 times, sc in next 16 st [68]

Rnd 17 – 22: sc in all 68 st [68]

Insert the safety eyes between rounds 15 and 16, with an interspace of 12 stitches. The marked part should be centered between the eyes. Using black embroidery thread, embroider the eyebrows on round 11. Each eyebrow is 1 stitch wide.

Rnd 23: sc in next 13 st, (sc in next st, dec) repeat 6 times, sc in next 4 st, (dec, sc in next st) repeat 6 times, sc in next 15 st [56]

Rnd 24: (sc in next 5 st, dec) repeat 8 times [48]

Rnd 25: (sc in next 4 st, dec) repeat 8 times [40]

Rnd 26: (sc in next 3 st, dec) repeat 8 times [32]

Rnd 27: (sc in next 2 st, dec) repeat 8 times [24]

Fasten off and weave in the yarn end. Stuff the head with fiberfill.

Next, we shape the nose and mouth (picture 3). Take a piece of pink yarn on your needle and bring the needle out in one of the marked stitches between rounds 15 and 16 (picture 4). Bring it back inside in the other marked stitch (picture 5). Bring the needle back out on round 19, centered below the pink stripe you've just made. Bring it back inside one stitch below and bring it out again in the first marked stitch (picture 6). Pull the yarn tight to shape the nose (picture 7). Make some extra horizontal stitches across the nose. Tie the yarn ends inside the head to finish. Sew the head

to the body, adding more fiberfill to the neck before closing the seam. Optionally, you can add pink makeup blush on the cheeks.

EAR (make 2, in brown yarn)

Rnd 1: start 6 sc in a magic ring [6]

Rnd 2: inc in all 6 st [12]

Rnd 3: (sc in next st, inc in next st) repeat 6 times [18]

Rnd 4: (sc in next 2 st, inc in next st) repeat 6 times [24]

Rnd 5: (sc in next 3 st, inc in next st) repeat 6 times [30]

Rnd 6: (sc in next 4 st, inc in next st) repeat 6 times [36]

Rnd 7 – 10: sc in all 36 st [36]

Rnd 11: (sc in next 4 st, dec) repeat 6 times [30]

Rnd 12 – 15: sc in all 30 st [30]

Rnd 16: (sc in next 3 st, dec) repeat 6 times [24]

Rnd 17 – 20: sc in all 24 st [24]

Fasten off, leaving a long yarn tail. The ears don't need to be stuffed. Flatten the base of the ear and sew it closed. Optionally, you can add pink makeup blush on the inside of the ear. Sew the ears to rounds 4-6 of the head.

ANTLER (make 2, in dark brown yarn)

Ch 9. Crochet in rows.

Row 1: start in second ch from hook, sc in next 3 st, ch 4, start in second ch from hook, slst in next 3 ch, slst in the same st on the foundation chain, sc in next 5 st. Fasten off. Sew the antlers in front of the ears. Make sure to mirror the left and right antler.

WREATH (in green yarn)

Ch 51. Crochet in rows.

Row 1: start in second ch from hook, (slst in next 3 st,
ch 4, start in second ch from hook, sc in this ch,
hdc inc in next ch, slst in next ch, slst in next 2 st on
the foundation chain) repeat 10 times.

Fasten off. Twist the wreath a few times and sew the
ends together. Position the wreath on top of the head
with pins and sew it on with a few stitches.

FLOWER (make 1 in pink, 1 in lilac and 1 in yellow yarn)

Ch 25. Crochet in rows.

Row 1: start in second ch from hook, slst in next 6 st,
sc in next 6 st, hdc in next 6 st, dc in next 6 st.

Fasten off, leaving a long tail for sewing. Starting with
the narrow end, roll up your work into a spiral and fix
it with a stitch to secure the flower in place. Sew the
flowers on top of the head on one side of the wreath
(picture 8).

grim reaper

A DESIGN BY MONSTERHOOK (ANNA CARAX)

The little Reaper may look scary, but don't be afraid, Grim is actually pretty easy-going and cool.
She loves goth fashion, loud music and dancing, so if you're hosting a party (even outside of Halloween),
don't hesitate to ask her over, she loves to shake her bones to the beat.

Skill level: ★ ★
Size: 8 in / 20 cm tall when
made with the indicated yarn

Amigurumi gallery: Scan or visit
www.amigurumi.com/4405
to share pictures and find inspiration.

YOU WILL NEED:
Fingering weight yarn
- ● black (2 balls)
- white
- ○ gray
- ● brown

Size B-1 / 2 mm crochet hook
Black felt (for the eyes)
Fabric glue
Metal wire / pipe cleaner
Scissors
Stitch markers
Yarn needle
Sewing needle
Fiberfill

HEAD (in white yarn)

Rnd 1: start 6 sc in a magic ring [6]
Rnd 2: inc in all 6 st [12]
Rnd 3: (sc in next st, inc in next st) repeat 6 times [18]
Rnd 4: sc in next st, inc in next st, (sc in next 2 st, inc in next st) repeat 5 times, sc in next st [24]
Rnd 5: (sc in next 3 st, inc in next st) repeat 6 times [30]
Rnd 6: sc in next 2 st, inc in next st, (sc in next 4 st, inc in next st) repeat 5 times, sc in next 2 st [36]
Rnd 7: (sc in next 5 st, inc in next st) repeat 6 times [42]
Rnd 8: sc in next 3 st, inc in next st, (sc in next 6 st, inc in next st) repeat 5 times, sc in next 3 st [48]

Rnd 9: (sc in next 7 st, inc in next st) repeat 6 times [54]
Rnd 10: sc in next 4 st, inc in next st, (sc in next 8 st, inc in next st) repeat 5 times, sc in next 4 st [60]
Rnd 11: (sc in next 9 st, inc in next st) repeat 6 times [66]
Rnd 12: sc in next 5 st, inc in next st, (sc in next 10 st, inc in next st) repeat 5 times, sc in next 5 st [72]
Rnd 13: (sc in next 11 st, inc in next st) repeat 6 times [78]
Rnd 14 – 27: sc in all 78 st [78]
Rnd 28: (sc in next 11 st, dec) repeat 6 times [72]
Rnd 29: sc in next 5 st, dec, (sc in next 10 st, dec) repeat 5 times, sc in next 5 st [66]
Rnd 30: (sc in next 9 st, dec) repeat 6 times [60]
Rnd 31: sc in next 4 st, dec, (sc in next 8 st, dec) repeat 5 times, sc in next 4 st [54]
Rnd 32: (sc in next 7 st, dec) repeat 6 times [48]
Rnd 33: sc in next 3 st, dec, (sc in next 6 st, dec) repeat 5 times, sc in next 3 st [42]
Rnd 34: (sc in next 5 st, dec) repeat 6 times [36]
Rnd 35: sc in next 2 st, dec, (sc in next 4 st, dec) repeat 5 times, sc in next 2 st [30]
Rnd 36: (sc in next 3 st, dec) repeat 6 times [24]
Slst in next st. Fasten off, leaving a long tail for sewing. Stuff the head with fiberfill. Cut 2 oval pieces of black felt (approx. 1 in / 2.5 cm in width and 1.2 in / 3 cm in height). Use fabric glue to glue them between rounds 17 and 25 of the head, with an interspace of 6 stitches. Embroider the mouth between rounds 25 and 29 of the head. Mark the smile with pins (picture 1) and embroider

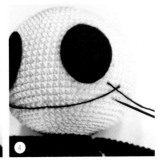

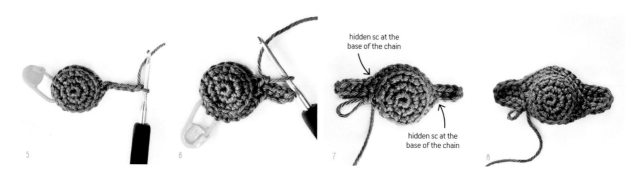

hidden sc at the base of the chain

hidden sc at the base of the chain

5   6   7   8

it with black embroidery thread or black yarn. First make the horizontal line (pictures 2-3) and then add small vertical lines crossing it (picture 4).

BODY (in black yarn)
Starting at the bottom.
Rnd 1: start 6 sc in a magic ring [6]
Rnd 2: inc in all 6 st [12]
Rnd 3: (sc in next st, inc in next st) repeat 6 times [18]
Rnd 4: BLO sc in all 18 st [18]
Rnd 5: (sc in next 9 st, ch 5 (picture 5), start in second ch from hook, sc in next 4 ch (picture 6), sc in same st at the base of the ch) repeat 2 times [38] (picture 7)
Rnd 6: (sc in next 3 st, inc in next st, sc in next 3 st, inc in next st, skip the hidden sc at the base of the chain (picture 7), sc in next 3 ch, inc in next ch, sc in next 5 st) repeat 2 times [40] (picture 8)
Rnd 7 – 18: sc in all 40 st [40]
Rnd 19: (sc in next 8 st, dec) repeat 4 times [36]
Rnd 20: sc in all 36 st [36]
Rnd 21: (sc in next 4 st, dec) repeat 6 times [30]
Rnd 22: (sc in next 3 st, dec) repeat 6 times [24]
Slst in next st. Fasten off and weave in the yarn end. Stuff the body with fiberfill (picture 9). Sew the head to the body.

ARM (make 2, start in white yarn)
Rnd 1: start 6 sc in a magic ring [6]

Rnd 2: (sc in next st, inc in next st) repeat 3 times [9]
Rnd 3: (sc in next 2 st, inc in next st) repeat 3 times [12]
Rnd 4: (sc in next 5 st, inc in next st) repeat 2 times [14]
Rnd 5: sc in next 7 st, 3-dc-bobble in next st, sc in next 6 st [14]
Rnd 6: (sc in next 5 st, dec) repeat 2 times [12]
Rnd 7: (sc in next 4 st, dec) repeat 2 times [10]
Change to black yarn. Stuff the arm with fiberfill and continue stuffing as you go. Stuff the last rounds lightly.
Rnd 8: (sc in next 4 st, inc in next st) repeat 2 times [12]
Rnd 9: (sc in next 5 st, inc in next st) repeat 2 times [14]
Rnd 10 – 17: sc in all 14 st [14]
Rnd 18: (sc in next 5 st, dec) repeat 2 times [12]
Slst in next st. Fasten off, leaving a long tail for sewing. Sew the arms to round 21 of the body.

LEG (make 2, in black yarn)
Rnd 1: start 6 sc in a magic ring [6]
Rnd 2: inc in all 6 st [12]
Rnd 3: (sc in next st, inc in next st) repeat 6 times [18]
Rnd 4: (sc in next 2 st, inc in next st) repeat 6 times [24]
Rnd 5: sc in all 24 st [24]
Stuff the leg with fiberfill and continue stuffing as you go.
Rnd 6: sc in next 9 st, dec 3 times, sc in next 9 st [21]
Rnd 7: sc in next 8 st, dec 3 times, sc in next 7 st [18]
Rnd 8 – 18: sc in all 18 st [18]
Rnd 19: (sc in next st, dec) repeat 6 times [12]

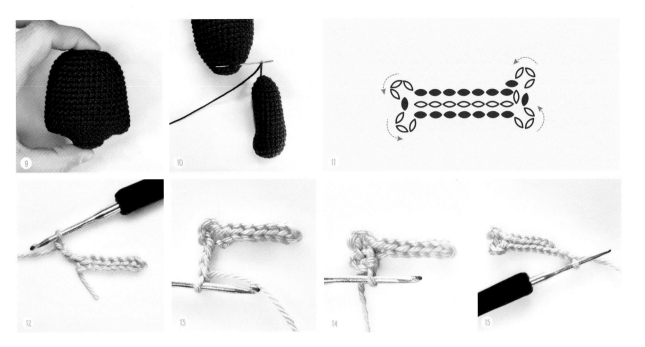

Rnd 20: dec 6 times [6]

Fasten off, leaving a long yarn tail. Using your yarn needle, weave the yarn tail through the front loop of each remaining stitch and pull it tight to close. Leave a yarn tail for sewing. Sew the legs between rounds 5-6 of the body (picture 10).

LEG BONE (make 2, in white yarn) (picture 11)
Ch 8. Stitches are worked around both sides of the foundation chain.
Rnd 1: start in second ch from hook, slst in next 6 st, slst + ch 3 + slst + ch 3 + slst in next st (pictures 12-14). Continue on the other side of the foundation chain, slst in next 5 st (picture 15), slst + ch 3 + slst + ch 3 in next st.
Slst in next st. Fasten off and weave in the yarn end.

ARM BONE (make 2, in white yarn)
Ch 6. Stitches are worked around both sides of the foundation chain.
Rnd 1: start in second ch from hook, slst in next 4 st, slst + ch 3 + slst + ch 3 + slst in next st. Continue on the other side of the foundation chain, slst in next 3 st, slst + ch 3 + slst + ch 3 in next st.
Slst in next st. Fasten off and weave in the yarn end.

RIBS (in white yarn)
Ch 10. The ribs are worked around both sides of this foundation chain. Do not fasten off between ribs.
Rib 1: start in second ch from hook, slst in next 2 st, ch 5 (picture 16), start in second ch from hook, slst in next 4 ch,
Rib 2: slst in next 3 st, ch 5 (picture 17), start in second ch from hook, slst in next 4 ch,
Rib 3: slst in next 3 st, ch 5, start in second ch from hook, slst in next 4 ch,
Rib 4: slst + hdc + slst + ch 5 in next st (picture 18), start in second ch from hook, slst in next 4 ch.
Continue on the other side of the foundation chain,

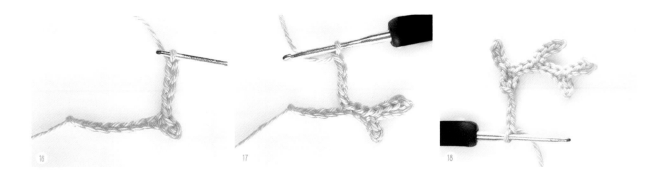

Rib 5: slst in next 3 st, ch 5, start in second ch from hook, slst in next 4 ch,
Rib 6: slst in next 3 st, ch 5, start in second ch from hook, slst in next 4 ch, slst in next 2 st.
Fasten off and weave in the yarn end.

HIP BONE 1 (in white yarn)
Ch 7. Crochet in rows.
Row 1: start in second ch from hook, sc in this st, hdc inc in next st, dc inc in next st, hdc inc in next st, sc in next st, slst in next st [9]
Fasten off and weave in the yarn end.

HIP BONE 2 (in white yarn)
Ch 7. Crochet in rows.
Row 1: start in second ch from hook, slst in this st, sc in next st, hdc inc in next st, dc inc in next st, hdc inc in next st, sc in next st [9]
Fasten off and weave in the yarn end. Use fabric glue to glue the bones to the Grim Reaper's body. Glue the hip bones between rounds 7-12, the leg bones between rounds 8-17, the arm bones between rounds 9-16 and the ribs between rounds 10-20.

CAPE

Hood (in black yarn)
Ch 35. Stitches are worked around both sides of the foundation chain. Work in rows.
Row 1: start in third ch from hook, hdc in next 33 st. Continue on the other side of the foundation chain, hdc in next 33 st, ch 2, turn [66]
Row 2 – 22: hdc in next 66 st, ch 2, turn [66] The hood is gradually taking shape, be careful to work in the last stitch at each row-end to create a straight edge.
Row 23: hdc in all 66 st, ch 1, turn [66]
Row 24: (sc in next st, dec) repeat 22 times, ch 1, turn [44]
Row 25: (sc in next 2 st, dec) repeat 11 times, ch 1, turn [33]
Row 26: sc in next 16 st, inc in next st, sc in next 16 st [34]
Fasten off, leaving a long tail for sewing.

Jacket (in black yarn)
Ch 36. Crochet in rows.
Row 1: start in third ch from hook, hdc in next 34 st, ch 2, turn [34]
In the next row, we'll leave spaces for the armholes.
Row 2: hdc in next 4 st, ch 12, skip 6 st, slst in next st, hdc in next 12 st, ch 12, skip 6 st, slst in next st, hdc in next 4 st, ch 2, turn [22 + 24 ch] (picture 19)
Row 3: hdc in next 4 st, skip the slst, hdc in next 12 ch, hdc in next 12 st, skip the slst, hdc in next 12 ch, hdc in next 4 st, ch 2, turn [44] (picture 20)
Row 4: hdc in all 44 st, ch 2, turn [44]

Row 5: (hdc in next 10 st, hdc inc in next st, hdc in next 5 st, hdc inc in next st) repeat 2 times, hdc in next 10 st, ch 2, turn [48]

Row 6: (hdc in next 7 st, hdc inc in next st) repeat 2 times, hdc in next 5 st, hdc inc in next st, hdc in next 4 st, hdc inc in next st, hdc in next 5 st, (hdc inc in next st, hdc in next 7 st) repeat 2 times, ch 2, turn [54]

Row 7 – 18: hdc in all 54 st, ch 2, turn [54]

Row 19: hdc in all 54 st [54]

Fasten off and weave in the yarn end.

Sleeve (make 2, in black yarn)

Hold the jacket with the outside toward you. Pull up a loop of black yarn in the outer right stitch of the armhole (picture 21).

Rnd 1: sc in next 9 st, sc in the corner space, sc in next 9 st, sc in next corner space [20]
Rnd 2: (hdc in next 9 st, hdc inc in next st) repeat 2 times [22]
Rnd 3 – 6: hdc in all 22 st [22]
Rnd 7: hdc in next 21 st, sc in next st [22]
Slst in next st. Fasten off and weave in the yarn end. Sew the bottom of the hood to the top side of the jacket. Put the cape on.

SCYTHE

Blade (in gray yarn)
Rnd 1: start 4 sc in a magic ring [4]
Rnd 2: (sc in next st, inc in next st) repeat 2 times [6]
Rnd 3: sc in all 6 st [6]
Rnd 4: inc in next 2 st, sc in next 2 st, inc in next 2 st [10]
Rnd 5: sc in all 10 st [10]
Rnd 6: inc in next 2 st, sc in next 6 st, inc in next 2 st [14]
Rnd 7: sc in all 14 st [14]
Rnd 8: inc in next 2 st, sc in next 2 st, dec 2 times, sc in next 4 st, inc in next 2 st [16]
Rnd 9: sc in all 16 st [16]
Rnd 10: inc in next 2 st, sc in next 2 st, dec 2 times, sc in next 6 st, inc in next 2 st [18]
Rnd 11: sc in all 18 st [18]
Rnd 12: inc in next 2 st, sc in next 4 st, dec 2 times, sc in next 6 st, inc in next 2 st [20]

Rnd 13: sc in all 20 st [20]
Rnd 14: inc in next 2 st, sc in next 5 st, dec 2 times, sc in next 7 st, inc in next 2 st [22]
Rnd 15: sc in all 22 st [22]
Rnd 16: inc in next 2 st, sc in next 5 st, dec 2 times, sc in next 9 st, inc in next 2 st [24]
Rnd 17: sc in all 24 st [24]
Rnd 18: inc in next 2 st, sc in next 6 st, dec 2 times, sc in next 10 st, inc in next 2 st [26]
Rnd 19: sc in all 26 st [26]
Rnd 20: inc in next 2 st, sc in next 5 st, dec 4 times, sc in next 9 st, inc in next 2 st [26]
Rnd 21: sc in all 26 st [26]
Rnd 22: inc in next 2 st, sc in next 5 st, dec 4 times, sc in next 9 st, inc in next 2 st [26]
Rnd 23: sc in all 26 st [26]
Rnd 24: inc in next 2 st, sc in next 5 st, dec 4 times, sc in next 9 st, inc in next 2 st [26]
Rnd 25: sc in all 26 st [26]
Rnd 26: inc in next 2 st, sc in next 5 st, dec 4 times, sc in next 9 st, inc in next 2 st [26]
Rnd 27: sc in all 26 st [26]
The blade doesn't need to be stuffed. Flatten the blade with the last stitch on the side and work the next round through both layers to close.
Rnd 28: sc in all 13 st, ch 1, turn [13] (picture 22)
Continue crocheting in rows.
Row 1: BLO sc in next 12 st, ch 1, turn [12] Leave the

remaining stitch unworked.
Row 2 – 9: sc in all 12 st, ch 1, turn [12]
Row 10: sc in all 12 st [12]
Fasten off, leaving a long tail for sewing (picture 23).

Handle (in brown yarn)
Rnd 1: start 7 sc in a magic ring [7]

Rnd 2 – 45: sc in all 7 st [7]
Insert a metal wire or pipe cleaner into the handle. Fasten off, leaving a long yarn tail. Using your yarn needle, weave the yarn tail through the front loop of each remaining stitch and pull it tight to close. Wrap the square part of the blade around the handle and sew it on (pictures 24-25).

Fuyuko
THE KITSUNE

A DESIGN BY PETITE PETALS

Meet Fuyuko, a benevolent celestial fox with nine tails that shine in the moonlight. With her magical powers and faithful nature, she protects shrines by warding off evil and works hard to help the local people. But don't let her demure appearance fool you, Fuyuko is a powerful shapeshifter who can transform into any creature she desires, from an old man to a majestic dragon. Her biggest weakness? Inari sushi!

Skill level: ★ ★ (★)
Size: 5 in / 12 cm tall when
made with the indicated yarn

Amigurumi gallery: Scan or visit
www.amigurumi.com/4406
to share pictures and find inspiration.

YOU WILL NEED:
Light worsted weight yarn
    white
    sky blue
Size C-2 / 2.5 mm crochet hook
Brown embroidery thread
Yarn needle
Embroidery needle
Pins
Poly pellets
Fiberfill
Optional: wire brush
Optional: red or pink makeup blush

HEAD (in white yarn)

Rnd 1: start 6 sc in magic ring [6]
Rnd 2: sc in next 3 st, inc in next 3 st [9]
Rnd 3: inc in next 3 st, sc in next 6 st [12]
Rnd 4: sc in next 6 st, (sc in next st, inc in next st) repeat 3 times [15]
Rnd 5: (sc in next st, inc in next st) repeat 3 times, sc in next 9 st [18]
Rnd 6: sc in all 18 st [18]
Rnd 7: (sc in next st, inc in next st) repeat 6 times, sc in next 6 st [24]
Rnd 8: (sc in next st, inc in next st) repeat 9 times, sc in next 6 st [33]
Rnd 9: sc in next 4 st, inc in next st, (sc in next 10 st, inc in next st) repeat 2 times, sc in next 6 st [36]
Rnd 10: (sc in next 11 st, inc in next st) repeat 3 times [39]
Rnd 11: sc in next 5 st, inc in next st, (sc in next 12 st, inc in next st) repeat 2 times, sc in next 7 st [42]
Rnd 12: (sc in next 13 st, inc in next st) repeat 2 times, sc in next 14 st [44]
Rnd 13: sc in next 4 st, dec, sc in next 30 st, dec, sc in next 6 st [42]

Rnd 14 – 19: sc in all 42 st [42]
Rnd 20: (sc in next 5 st, dec) repeat 6 times [36]
Rnd 21: (sc in next 4 st, dec) repeat 6 times [30]
Stuff the head with fiberfill and continue stuffing as you go.
Rnd 22: (sc in next 3 st, dec) repeat 6 times [24]
Rnd 23: (sc in next 2 st, dec) repeat 6 times [18]
Rnd 24: (sc in next st, dec) repeat 6 times [12]
Rnd 25: dec 6 times [6]
Fasten off, leaving a yarn tail. Using your yarn needle, weave the yarn tail through the front loop of each remaining stitch and pull it tight to close. Weave in the yarn end.

EAR (make 2, in white yarn)

Rnd 1: start 6 sc in magic ring [6]
Rnd 2: (sc in next st, inc in next st) repeat 3 times [9]
Rnd 3: (sc in next 2 st, inc in next st) repeat 3 times [12]
Rnd 4: (sc in next 3 st, inc in next st) repeat 3 times [15]

Rnd 5: (sc in next 4 st, inc in next st) repeat 3 times [18]
Rnd 6: (sc in next 5 st, inc in next st) repeat 3 times [21]
Rnd 7 – 9: sc in all 21 st [21]
Fasten off, leaving a long tail for sewing. Flatten the ears and pinch them at the bottom. Pin the ears to the head, with the front corners of the ear on round 13 and the back side on round 17. Sew the ears to the head (picture 1). Optionally, add a bit of red or pink makeup blush on the inside of the ears.
Embroider the nose using brown embroidery thread. Make a small triangle over round 1 (picture 2) and fill it in with vertical lines. Embroider the eyes with brown embroidery thread. Embroider a straight line twice from round 6 to round 10 (picture 3) and gently tug the straight line upward at round 9, to create an arch. Use one strand of brown embroidery thread to sew over the arch to hold it in place (picture 4). The inside corners of the eyes should be 5 stitches apart. Embroider the head markings using sky blue yarn. Embroider a straight line in the center of the head, from round 8 to 12. Skip one stitch to the left of the line and sew a shorter straight line from round 8 to 10. Embroider another short line to the right side of the center line. Sew each line around one more time to thicken the markings (picture 5).

FRONT LEGS (make 2, in white yarn)
Rnd 1: start 6 sc in magic ring [6]
Rnd 2: (3 sc in next st, inc in next st, sc in next st) repeat 2 times [12]
Rnd 3: BLO sc in all 12 st [12]
Rnd 4 – 5: sc in all 12 st [12]
Rnd 6: dec 3 times, sc in next 6 st [9]
Rnd 7 – 10: sc in all 9 st [9]
Fasten off, leaving a long tail for sewing.

BODY (in white yarn)
Rnd 1: start 6 sc in magic ring [6]
Rnd 2: inc in all 6 st [12]
Rnd 3: (sc in next st, inc in next st) repeat 6 times [18]
Rnd 4: (sc in next 2 st, inc in next st) repeat 6 times [24]
Rnd 5: (sc in next 3 st, inc in next st) repeat 6 times [30]
Rnd 6 – 8: sc in all 30 st [30]
Rnd 9: sc in next 15 st, (sc in next 4 st, inc in next st) repeat 3 times [33]
Rnd 10: sc in all 33 st [33]
Rnd 11: sc in next 15 st, (sc in next 5 st, inc in next st) repeat 3 times [36]
Rnd 12: sc in all 36 st [36]
Stuff the legs with fiberfill. In the next round, we will join the front legs to the body. Make sure that the feet

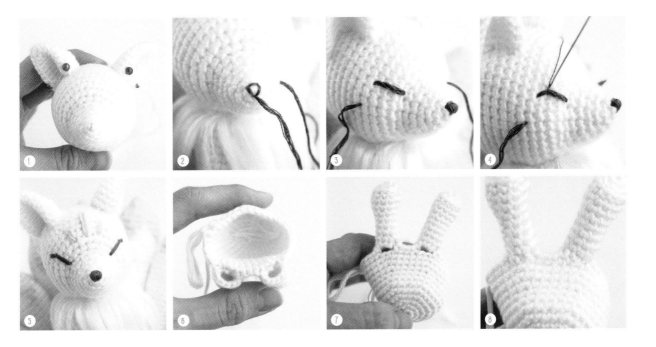

are pointing forward when joining the legs.

Rnd 13: (sc in next 4 st, dec) repeat 3 times, sc in next 4 st, continue in first st of Rnd 10 of the first front leg: sc in next 7 st on the leg, skip 2 st on the body, sc in next 4 st on the body, continue in first st of Rnd 10 of the second front leg: sc in next 7 st on the leg, skip 2 st on the body, sc in next 6 st on the body [43] (picture 6)

There will be a gap between each leg and the body (picture 7). Sew the gaps closed using the yarn tails of the front legs (picture 8).

Rnd 14: sc in next 26 st, dec, sc in next 15 st [42]

Rnd 15: sc in next 5 st, dec, sc in next 12 st, dec, sc in next 4 st, dec, sc in next 5 st, dec, sc in next 8 st [38]

Rnd 16: sc in all 38 st [38]

Rnd 17: sc in next 17 st, dec, sc in next 10 st, dec, sc in next 7 st [36]

Rnd 18 – 20: sc in all 36 st [36]

Rnd 21: sc in next 4 st, dec, (sc in next 10 st, dec)

repeat 2 times, sc in next 6 st [33]

Rnd 22: sc in all 33 st [33]

Rnd 23: (sc in next 9 st, dec) repeat 3 times [30]

Rnd 24: (sc in next 3 st, dec) repeat 6 times [24]

Rnd 25: sc in next st, hdc in next st, dc in next 3 st, tr in next 2 st, dc in next 3 st, hdc in next st, sc in next st [12]

Leave the remaining stitches unworked.

Fasten off, leaving a long tail for sewing. You can add approx. 8 g of poly pellets to the body before you stuff it with fiberfill, this will help the kitsune to sit upright. Put the pellets into an old panty or sock before inserting it into the body. Stuff the body with fiberfill.

To make the fur around the neck, cut 24 strands of white yarn (3 in / 8 cm in length). Pull each strand through a loop of round 25, knotting to secure it (pictures 9-10). Brush the fur around the neck with a wire brush to make it fluffy and trim it to your liking (picture 11).

Pin and sew the head to the body, adding more fiberfill to the neck before closing the seam.

HIND LEG (in white yarn)

Foot (make 2)
Rnd 1: start 6 sc in magic ring [6]
Rnd 2: (sc in next st, inc in next st) repeat 3 times [9]
Rnd 3 – 4: sc in all 9 st [9]
Stuff the foot with fiberfill. Fasten off, leaving a long tail for sewing.

Haunch (make 2)
Rnd 1: start 6 sc in magic ring [6]
Rnd 2: inc in all 6 st [12]
Rnd 3: (sc in next st, inc in next st) repeat 6 times [18]
Rnd 4 – 9: sc in all 18 st [18]
Stuff the haunch lightly with fiberfill and continue stuffing as you go.
Rnd 10: (sc in next st, dec) repeat 6 times [12]
Rnd 11: dec 6 times [6]
Fasten off, leaving a long tail for sewing. Using your yarn needle, weave the yarn tail through the front loop of each remaining stitch and pull it tight to close. Leave a long tail for sewing. Flatten the haunch and sew the foot and haunch together (picture 12). Position and sew the hind legs to the sides of the body.

TAILS
Note: If you find it challenging to work with two yarn colors, you have the option to disregard the color changes in the tail.

Tail 1 (start in sky blue yarn)
Rnd 1: start 4 sc in magic ring [4]
Rnd 2: sc in next st, inc in next 3 st [7]
Rnd 3: sc in next st, (sc in next st, inc in next st) repeat 3 times [10]
Rnd 4: sc in next st, (sc in next st, inc in next st) repeat 4 times, sc in next st [14]
Rnd 5: (sc in next 2 st, inc in next st) repeat 4 times, sc in next 2 st [18]
Rnd 6: sc in next 3 st, (sc in next 3 st, inc in next st) repeat 3 times, sc in next 3 st [21]
Work the next rounds with alternating colors. The color changes are indicated in italics.
Rnd 7: sc in next 7 st, inc in next st, sc in next 2 st, *(white)* sc in next st, *(sky blue)* sc in next st, inc in next st, sc in next st, *(white)* sc in next st, *(sky blue)* sc in next 2 st, inc in next st, *(white)* sc in next st, *(sky blue)* sc in next 2 st [24]
Note: in round 8 you work 2 increase stitches with one sky blue and one white stitch. Be careful to work the stitch in the same stitch, as mentioned.
Rnd 8: sc in next st, *(white)* sc in next st, *(sky blue)* sc in next 3 st, *(white)* sc in next st, *(sky blue)* sc in next

3 st, *(white)* sc in <u>same</u> st, *(sky blue)* sc in next 2 st, *(white)* sc in next 2 st, *(sky blue)* sc in next st, inc in next st, *(white)* sc in next 3 st, *(sky blue)* sc in next 3 st, *(white)* sc in <u>same</u> st, sc in next 2 st, *(sky blue)* sc in next st [27]

Rnd 9: *(white)* sc in next 3 st, *(sky blue)* sc in next 2 st, *(white)* sc in next 2 st, *(sky blue)* sc in next st, *(white)* sc in next 3 st, *(sky blue)* sc in next st, *(white)* sc in next 3 st, *(sky blue)* sc in next st, *(white)* sc in next 5 st, *(sky blue)* sc in next st, *(white)* sc in next 5 st [27]
Continue in white yarn.

Rnd 10: (sc in next st, dec) repeat 3 times, (sc in next 5 st, inc in next st) repeat 3 times [27]

Rnd 11: sc in all 27 st [27]

Rnd 12: (sc in next st, dec) repeat 2 times, (sc in next 5 st, inc in next st) repeat 3 times, sc in next st, dec [27]

Rnd 13: sc in all 27 st [27]

Rnd 14: (sc in next 7 st, dec) repeat 3 times [24]

Rnd 15: sc in next 4 st, dec, (sc in next 5 st, inc in next st) repeat 2 times, sc in next 4 st, dec [24]

Rnd 16: sc in all 24 st [24]

Rnd 17: sc in next 2 st, dec, (sc in next 6 st, dec) repeat 2 times, sc in next 4 st [21]

Rnd 18: sc in all 21 st [21]
Stuff the tail with fiberfill and continue stuffing as you go.

Rnd 19: (sc in next 5 st, dec) repeat 3 times [18]

Rnd 20: sc in all 18 st [18]

Rnd 21: (sc in next 7 st, dec) repeat 2 times [16]

Rnd 22 — 23: sc in all 16 st [16]

Rnd 24: (sc in next 2 st, dec, sc in next 4 st) repeat 2 times [14]

Rnd 25 — 26: sc in all 14 st [14]

Rnd 27: (sc in next 5 st, dec) repeat 2 times [12]

Rnd 28 — 30: sc in all 12 st [12]

Rnd 31: (sc in next st, dec, sc in next 3 st) repeat 2 times [10]

Rnd 32: sc in all 10 st [10]

Rnd 33: (sc in next 3 st, dec) repeat 2 times [8]

Rnd 34: sc in all 8 st [8]

Rnd 35: (sc in next 2 st, dec) repeat 2 times [6]

Rnd 36: sc in all 6 st [6]

Rnd 37: (sc in next st, dec) repeat 2 times [4]
Fasten off, leaving a long tail for sewing.

Tail 2/3 (make 2, start in sky blue yarn)

Rnd 1 — 7: repeat the pattern for tail 1.

Rnd 8: sc in next st, *(white)* sc in next st, *(sky blue)* sc in next 4 st, *(white)* sc in next st, *(sky blue)* sc in next 3 st, *(white)* sc in next 3 st, *(sky blue)* sc in next 2 st, *(white)* sc in next 3 st, *(sky blue)* sc in next 2 st, *(white)* sc in next 3 st, *(sky blue)* sc in next st [24]

Rnd 9: *(white)* sc in next 3 st, *(sky blue)* sc in next st, dec, *(white)* sc in next 2 st, *(sky blue)* sc in next st, *(white)* sc in next 2 st, inc in next st, sc in next 2 st,

(sky blue) sc in next st, *(white)* sc in next 2 st, inc in next st, sc in next st, *(sky blue)* sc in next st, *(white)* sc in next 2 st, dec [24]
Continue in white yarn.
Rnd 10: sc in all 24 st [24]
Rnd 11: (sc in next st, dec) repeat 2 times, (sc in next 4 st, inc in next st) repeat 3 times, sc in next st, dec [24]
Rnd 12: sc in all 24 st [24]
Rnd 13: sc in next 2 st, dec, (sc in next 6 st, dec) repeat 2 times, sc in next 4 st [21]
Rnd 14: sc in all 21 st [21]
Rnd 15: sc in next 2 st, dec, (sc in next 5 st, inc in next st) repeat 2 times, sc in next 3 st, dec [21]
Rnd 16: sc in all 21 st [21]
Stuff the tail with fiberfill and continue stuffing as you go.
Rnd 17: (sc in next 5 st, dec) repeat 3 times [18]
Rnd 18: sc in all 18 st [18]
Rnd 19: (sc in next 7 st, dec) repeat 2 times [16]
Rnd 20 – 21: sc in all 16 st [16]
Rnd 22: (sc in next 2 st, dec, sc in next 4 st) repeat 2 times [14]
Rnd 23 – 24: sc in all 14 st [14]
Rnd 25: (sc in next 5 st, dec) repeat 2 times [12]
Rnd 26 – 28: sc in all 12 st [12]
Rnd 29: (sc in next st, dec, sc in next 3 st) repeat 2 times [10]
Rnd 30: sc in all 10 st [10]
Rnd 31: (sc in next 3 st, dec) repeat 2 times [8]
Rnd 32: sc in all 8 st [8]
Rnd 33: (sc in next 2 st, dec) repeat 2 times [6]
Rnd 34: sc in all 6 st [6]
Rnd 35: (sc in next st, dec) repeat 2 times [4]
Fasten off, leaving a long tail for sewing.

Tail 4/5 (make 2, start in sky blue yarn)
Rnd 1 – 7: repeat the pattern for tail 1.

Rnd 8: sc in next st, *(white)* sc in next st, *(sky blue)* sc in next 4 st, *(white)* sc in next st, *(sky blue)* sc in next 3 st, *(white)* sc in next 3 st, *(sky blue)* sc in next 2 st, *(white)* sc in next 3 st, *(sky blue)* sc in next 2 st, *(white)* sc in next 3 st, *(sky blue)* sc in next st [24]
Note: in round 9 you work 2 increase stitches with one white and one sky blue stitch. Be careful to work the stitch in the same stitch, as mentioned.
Rnd 9: *(white)* sc in next st, dec, *(sky blue)* sc in next st, dec, *(white)* sc in next st, dec, *(sky blue)* sc in next st, *(white)* sc in next 4 st *(sky blue)* sc in <u>same</u> st, *(white)* sc in next 5 st, *(sky blue)* sc in <u>same</u> st, *(white)* sc in next 4 st, inc in next st [24]
Continue in white yarn.
Rnd 10: sc in all 24 st [24]
Rnd 11: sc in next 2 st, dec, (sc in next 6 st, dec) repeat 2 times, sc in next 4 st [21]
Rnd 12: sc in next 2 st, dec, (sc in next 5 st, inc in next st) repeat 2 times, sc in next 3 st, dec [21]
Rnd 13: sc in all 21 st [21]
Stuff the tail with fiberfill and continue stuffing as you go.
Rnd 14: (sc in next 5 st, dec) repeat 3 times [18]
Rnd 15: sc in all 18 st [18]
Rnd 16: (sc in next 7 st, dec) repeat 2 times [16]
Rnd 17: sc in all 16 st [16]
Rnd 18: (sc in next 2 st, dec, sc in next 4 st) repeat 2 times [14]
Rnd 19 – 20: sc in all 14 st [14]
Rnd 21: (sc in next 5 st, dec) repeat 2 times [12]
Rnd 22 – 23: sc in all 12 st [12]
Rnd 24: (sc in next st, dec, sc in next 3 st) repeat 2 times[10]
Rnd 25: sc in all 10 st [10]
Rnd 26: (sc in next 3 st, dec) repeat 2 times [8]
Rnd 27: sc in all 8 st [8]
Rnd 28: (sc in next 2 st, dec) repeat 2 times [6]

Rnd 29: sc in all 6 st [6]
Rnd 30: (sc in next st, dec) repeat 2 times [4]
Fasten off, leaving a long tail for sewing.

Tail 6/7 (make 2, start in sky blue yarn)
Rnd 1 – 5: repeat the pattern for tail 1.
Work the next rounds with alternating colors. The color changes are indicated in italics.
Rnd 6: sc in next 6 st, inc in next st, sc in next 2 st, *(white)* sc in next st, *(sky blue)* inc in next st, sc in next 2 st, *(white)* sc in next st, *(sky blue)* inc in next st, sc in next st, *(white)* sc in next st, *(sky blue)* sc in next st [21]
Rnd 7: sc in next 2 st, *(white)* sc in next st, *(sky blue)* sc in next 3 st, *(white)* sc in next st, *(sky blue)* sc in next 2 st, *(white)* sc in next 3 st, *(sky blue)* sc in next 2 st, *(white)* sc in next 3 st, *(sky blue)* sc in next 2 st, *(white)* sc in next 2 st [21]
Rnd 8: *(sky blue)* sc in next st, *(white)* dec, sc in next st, *(sky blue)* dec, *(white)* sc in next st, *(sky blue)* dec, *(white)* sc in next 3 st, inc in next st, *(sky blue)* sc in next st, *(white)* sc in next 2 st, inc in next st, sc in next 3 st, inc in next st [21]
Continue in white yarn.
Rnd 9: sc in all 21 st [21]
Stuff the tail with fiberfill and continue stuffing as you go.
Rnd 10: (sc in next 5 st, dec) repeat 3 times [18]
Rnd 11: sc in all 18 st [18]
Rnd 12: (sc in next 7 st, dec) repeat 2 times [16]
Rnd 13: sc in all 16 st [16]
Rnd 14: (sc in next 2 st, dec, sc in next 4 st) repeat 2 times [14]
Rnd 15: sc in all 14 st [14]
Rnd 16: (sc in next 5 st, dec) repeat 2 times [12]
Rnd 17: sc in all 12 st [12]
Rnd 18: (sc in next st, dec, sc in next 3 st) repeat 2 times [10]
Rnd 19: sc in all 10 st [10]
Rnd 20: (sc in next 3 st, dec) repeat 2 times [8]
Rnd 21: sc in all 8 st [8]
Rnd 22: (sc in next 2 st, dec) repeat 2 times [6]
Rnd 23: sc in all 6 st [6]
Rnd 24: (sc in next st, dec) repeat 2 times [4]
Fasten off, leaving a long tail for sewing.

Tail 8/9 (make 2, start in sky blue yarn)
Rnd 1 – 4: repeat the pattern for tail 1.
Rnd 5: sc in next st, dec, (sc in next 3 st, inc in next st) repeat 2 times, sc in next st, dec [14]
Work the next rounds with alternating colors. The color changes are indicated in italics.
Rnd 6: sc in next 2 st, *(white)* sc in next st, *(sky blue)* sc in next 3 st, *(white)* sc in next st, *(sky blue)* sc in next

3 st, *(white)* sc in next st, *(sky blue)* sc in next
2 st, *(white)* sc in next st [14]

Rnd 7: *(sky blue)* sc in next st, *(white)* sc in next
3 st, *(sky blue)* sc in next st, *(white)* sc in next 3 st,
(sky blue) sc in next st, *(white)* sc in next 3 st, *(sky
blue)* sc in next st, *(white)* sc in next st [14]
Continue in white yarn.

Rnd 8 – 10: sc in all 14 st [14]
Stuff the tail with fiberfill and continue stuffing as

you go.

Rnd 11: (sc in next 5 st, dec) repeat 2 times [12]

Rnd 12: (sc in next st, dec, sc in next 3 st) repeat
2 times [10]

Rnd 13: sc in all 10 st [10]

Rnd 14: (sc in next 3 st, dec) repeat 2 times [8]

Rnd 15: sc in all 8 st [8]

Rnd 16: (sc in next 2 st, dec) repeat 2 times [6]

Rnd 17: sc in all 6 st [6]

Rnd 18: (sc in next st, dec) repeat 2 times [4]
Fasten off, leaving a long tail for sewing. Brush the
nine tails with a wire brush to make them fluffy. Sew
the tails tightly together, according to the sequence
9 – 7 – 5 – 3 – 1 – 2 – 4 – 6 – 8 (picture 13). Make sure
to sew across all the tails in the middle and at the bottom.
Pin and sew the tails to the back of the body. Make sure
to test the balance of your kitsune before sewing the
tails to the body.

Aridae
THE WOODLAND PIXIE

A DESIGN BY AMIGURUMEANDO CON LA LUNA (LÚA MARTÍNEZ)

As a woodland pixie, Aridae loves nature. It can be very hard to find her, since she loves to hide and blend in with her natural surroundings. Her dress is made of tree bark, leaves and flowers, and the only thing that might give away her hiding spot is her mischievous laugh ringing through the forest.

Skill level: ★ ★
Size: 8 in / 21 cm when made with the indicated yarn

Amigurumi gallery: Scan or visit
www.amigurumi.com/4407
to share pictures and find inspiration.

YOU WILL NEED:
Fingering weight yarn
- skin color of your choice
- off-white
- green
- brown
- light brown (leftover)
- red
- orange

Sizes 2 mm, 2.25 mm and 2.5 mm crochet hooks
Safety eyes (6 mm)
Sewing needle
Stitch markers
Fiberfill
Optional: dark pink makeup blush

Note: Use a 2 mm crochet hook, unless the pattern states otherwise.

HEAD (in skin color yarn)
Rnd 1: start 6 sc in a magic ring [6]
Rnd 2: inc in all 6 st [12]
Rnd 3: (sc in next st, inc in next st) repeat 6 times [18]
Rnd 4: (sc in next 2 st, inc in next st) repeat 6 times [24]
Rnd 5: (sc in next 3 st, inc in next st) repeat 6 times [30]
Rnd 6: (sc in next 4 st, inc in next st) repeat 6 times [36]
Rnd 7: (sc in next 5 st, inc in next st) repeat 6 times [42]
Rnd 8: (sc in next 6 st, inc in next st) repeat 6 times [48]
Rnd 9: (sc in next 7 st, inc in next st) repeat 6 times [54]
Rnd 10: (sc in next 8 st, inc in next st) repeat 6 times [60]
Rnd 11: (sc in next 9 st, inc in next st) repeat 6 times [66]
Rnd 12 – 24: sc in all 66 st [66]
Rnd 25: (dec, sc in next 9 st) repeat 6 times [60]
Rnd 26: (dec, sc in next 8 st) repeat 6 times [54]
Rnd 27: (dec, sc in next 7 st) repeat 6 times [48]
Insert the safety eyes between rounds 21 and 22, with an interspace of 12 stitches.

Rnd 28: (dec, sc in next 6 st) repeat 6 times [42]
Rnd 29: (dec, sc in next 5 st) repeat 6 times [36]
Rnd 30: (dec, sc in next 4 st) repeat 6 times [30]
Rnd 31: (dec, sc in next 3 st) repeat 6 times [24]
Rnd 32: (dec, sc in next 2 st) repeat 6 times [18]
Rnd 33: (dec, sc in next 4 st) repeat 3 times [15]
Slst in next st. Fasten off and weave in the yarn end.
Stuff the head firmly with fiberfill.

EAR (make 2, in skin color yarn)
Rnd 1: start 4 sc in a magic ring [4]
Rnd 2: (sc in next st, inc in next st) repeat 2 times [6]
Rnd 3: sc in all 6 st [6]
Rnd 4: (sc in next st, inc in next st) repeat 3 times [9]
Rnd 5: sc in all 9 st [9]
Rnd 6: (sc in next st, inc in next st) repeat 4 times,
sc in next st [13]
Rnd 7: sc in all 13 st [13]
Rnd 8: (sc in next st, inc in next st) repeat 6 times,
sc in next st [19]
Rnd 9 – 11: sc in all 19 st [19]
Rnd 12: (dec, sc in next st) repeat 6 times, sc in
next st [13]
Fasten off, leaving a long tail for sewing. The ears
don't need to be stuffed.

HAIR (in brown yarn)
Rnd 1: start 6 sc in a magic ring [6]

Rnd 2: inc in all 6 st [12]
Rnd 3: (sc in next st, inc in next st) repeat 6 times [18]
Rnd 4: (sc in next 2 st, inc in next st) repeat 6 times [24]
Rnd 5: (sc in next 3 st, inc in next st) repeat 6 times [30]
In the next round, we'll make the hair strands.
Rnd 6: (slst in next st, ch 65 (picture 1), start in second
ch from hook, sc in all 64 ch (picture 2)) repeat 30
times [30 strands]
Slst in same st. Fasten off, leaving a long tail for sewing.
Twirl each strand from tip to root to curl them (picture 3).
Position the hair to the head. Pin the magic ring of the
hair to the magic ring of the head (picture 4). Pin the hair
strands to the head and position them on both sides of
the face (picture 5) and around the head (pictures 6-7).
Sew each hair strand on (attach it until you reach the pin
and leave the rest of each strand free) (picture 8).
Pinch the ears and sew them closed with a few stitches
(picture 9). Sew the ears on both sides of the head, at
approx. 8 stitches from the eyes and two rounds below
them (picture 10). The ears should point downward.

ARM (make 2, in skin color yarn)
Rnd 1: start 6 sc in a magic ring [6]
Rnd 2: inc in all 6 st [12]
Rnd 3 – 5: sc in all 12 st [12]
Rnd 6: (dec, sc in next 4 st) repeat 2 times [10]
Rnd 7 – 25: sc in all 10 st [10]
Stuff the arm lightly with fiberfill. Flatten the opening

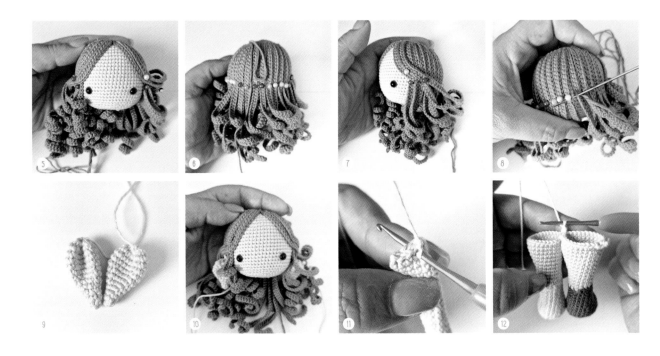

of the arm with the last stitch on the side and work the next round through both layers to close (picture 11).
Rnd 26: sc in next 5 st [5]
Fasten off, leaving a long tail for sewing.

LEG (make 2, start in off-white yarn for the first leg and green yarn for the second leg)
Rnd 1: start 6 sc in a magic ring [6]
Rnd 2: inc in all 6 st [12]
Rnd 3: (sc in next st, inc in next st) repeat 6 times [18]
Rnd 4: (sc in next 2 st, inc in next st) repeat 6 times [24]
Rnd 5: BLO sc in all 24 st [24]
Rnd 6 – 8: sc in all 24 st [24]
Rnd 9: sc in next 8 st, dec 4 times, sc in next 8 st [20]
Rnd 10: sc in next 8 st, dec 2 times, sc in next 8 st [18]
Rnd 11: sc in next 8 st, dec, sc in next 8 st [17]
Rnd 12 – 15: sc in all 17 st [17]
Change to skin color yarn. Stuff the legs with fiberfill and continue stuffing as you go.

Rnd 16: BLO sc in all 17 st [17]
Rnd 17 – 20: sc in all 17 st [17]
Rnd 21: sc in next 4 st, inc in next st, sc in next 7 st, inc in next st, sc in next 4 st [19]
Rnd 22: sc in all 19 st [19]
Rnd 23: sc in next 5 st, inc in next st, sc in next 7 st, inc in next st, sc in next 5 st [21]
Rnd 24: sc in all 21 st [21]
Rnd 25: sc in next 6 st, inc in next st, sc in next 7 st, inc in next st, sc in next 6 st [23]
Rnd 26 – 27: sc in all 23 st [23]
Rnd 28: inc in next st, sc in next 22 st [24]
Fasten off and weave in the yarn end. In the next round, we'll join the legs together to make the body.

BODY (continue in white yarn)
Position the legs with the feet facing forward. Mark the inner center stitch of both legs. Insert the hook through both center stitches, pull up a loop of white yarn

and join the marked stitches with a slst (picture 12).
Rnd 29: ch 1, sc in next 24 st on the first leg, sc in next 24 st on the second leg [48] (picture 13)
Rnd 30: (sc in next 7 st, inc in next st) repeat 6 times [54]
Rnd 31: (sc in next 8 st, inc in next st) repeat 6 times [60]
Rnd 32 − 34: sc in all 60 st [60]
Rnd 35: (dec, sc in next 8 st) repeat 6 times [54]
Rnd 36 − 37: sc in all 54 st [54]
Change to skin color yarn. Stuff the body with fiberfill and continue stuffing as you go.
Rnd 38: BLO sc in all 54 st [54]
Rnd 39: (dec, sc in next 7 st) repeat 6 times [48]
Rnd 40 − 42: sc in all 48 st [48]
Rnd 43: (dec, sc in next 6 st) repeat 6 times [42]
Rnd 44 − 46: sc in all 42 st [42]
Rnd 47: (dec, sc in next 5 st) repeat 6 times [36]
Rnd 48 − 54: sc in all 36 st [36]
Rnd 55: (dec, sc in next 4 st) repeat 6 times [30]
Rnd 56: (dec, sc in next 3 st) repeat 6 times [24]

Rnd 57: (dec, sc in next 2 st) repeat 6 times [18]
Rnd 58: (dec, sc in next 4 st) repeat 3 times [15]
Rnd 59 − 60: sc in all 15 st [15]
Fasten off, leaving a long tail for sewing. Sew the head to the body (picture 14). Add more fiberfill to the neck before closing the seam. Sew the arms to the body, 5 rounds below the last round of the neck (picture 15). Embroider a belly button with skin color yarn, 2 rounds above the panties (picture 16). Embroider two lines on each sock (using green yarn on the white sock and white yarn on the green sock) (picture 17). Add a bit of makeup blush across the face and on the inner part of the ears (picture 18).

TOP (in orange yarn)
Ch 25. Crochet in rows.
Row 1: start in second ch from hook, sc in next 24 ch, ch 1, turn [24]
Row 2: (sc in next st, inc in next st) repeat 12 times,

ch 1, turn [36]

Row 3: sc in next 5 st, ch 6 (picture 19), skip 6 st (picture 20), sc in next 14 st, ch 6, skip 6 st, sc in next 5 st, ch 1, turn [24 + 12 ch]

Row 4: sc in next 5 st, sc in next 6 ch, sc in next 14 st, sc in next 6 ch, sc in next 5 st, ch 1, turn [36] (picture 21)

Row 5: (sc in next 5 st, inc in next st) repeat 6 times, ch 1, turn [42]

Row 6: sc in all 42 st, ch 1, turn [42]

Row 7: (sc in next 6 st, inc in next st) repeat 6 times, ch 1, turn [48]

Row 8 – 9: sc in all 48 st, ch 1, turn [48]

Row 10: sc in all 48 st [48]

Fasten off, leaving a long tail for sewing (picture 22).

LEAF (make 9, in green yarn)

Ch 5. Stitches are worked around both sides of the foundation chain.

Rnd 1: start in second ch from hook, inc in this st, hdc inc in next st, sc in next st, slst in next st, ch 2. Continue on the other side of the foundation chain and skip the ch 2 you just made, slst in next st, sc in next st, hdc inc in next st, inc in next st [12]

Fasten off, leaving a long tail for sewing. Sew the leaves to the lower side of the top with an interspace of approx. 5 stitches (picture 23). Put the top on your doll and sew the back part closed (picture 24).

TROUSERS

Trouser leg (make 2, in red yarn)

Ch 27 and join with a slst to make a circle.

Rnd 1: sc in all 27 st [27]

Rnd 2: BLO sc in all 27 st [27]

Fasten off and weave in the yarn end on the first trouser leg. Don't fasten off on the second trouser leg.

Joining the trouser legs together

Join both trouser legs together with a slst (picture 25).

Rnd 3: sc in next 27 st on the first trouser leg, sc in next 27 st on the second trouser leg [54]

Rnd 4: BLO sc in all 54 st [54]

Rnd 5: sc in all 54 st [54]

Rnd 6: BLO sc in all 54 st [54]

Rnd 7: sc in all 54 st [54]

Rnd 8: BLO sc in all 54 st [54]

Rnd 9: sc in all 54 st [54]

Rnd 10: BLO sc in all 54 st [54]

Rnd 11: sc in all 54 st [54]

Rnd 12: BLO sc in all 54 st [54]

Rnd 13: sc in next st, (ch 3, sc in next st) repeat 53 times. Fasten off and weave in the yarn end (picture 26).

Pull up a loop of red yarn in the last leftover front loop of round 11.

Work in the leftover front loops of Rnd 11, 9, 7, 5, 3, 1: FLO sc in next st, (ch 3, sc in next st) repeat 53 times (picture 27).

Fasten off and weave in the yarn end.

SHOE (make 2, start in light brown yarn, with a 2.25 mm crochet hook)

Rnd 1: start 6 sc in a magic ring [6]

Rnd 2: inc in all 6 st [12]

Rnd 3: (sc in next st, inc in next st) repeat 6 times [18]

Rnd 4: (sc in next 2 st, inc in next st) repeat 6 times [24]

Change to brown yarn.

Rnd 5: BLO sc in all 24 st [24]

Rnd 6 – 9: sc in all 24 st [24]

Rnd 10: sc in next 8 st, dec 4 times, sc in next 8 st [20]

Rnd 11: FLO slst in next 7 st, ch 7, skip 7 st, FLO slst in next 6 st [13 + 7 ch] (picture 28)

Fasten off and weave in the yarn end.

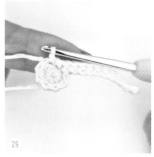

FLOWER

Petals (make 2, in off-white yarn, with a 2.5 mm crochet hook)
Rnd 1: start 8 sc in a magic ring [8]
Rnd 2: sc in all 8 st [8]
Rnd 3: (slst in next st, ch 11, start in second ch from hook, sc in all 10 ch, slst in same st as first slst (picture 29), ch 1) repeat 8 times [8 petals] (picture 30)
Work the next round around all petals.
Rnd 4: start in the first st of the petal (picture 31), (slst in next st, sc in next st, hdc in next 7 st, hdc inc in next st. Continue on the other side of the petal, hdc inc in next st, hdc in next 7 st, sc in next st, slst in next st, slst in the ch-space of Rnd 3) repeat 8 times [8 petals] (picture 32)
Fasten off and weave in the yarn end on one flower. Leave a long tail for sewing on the second flower.

Flower heart (in green yarn, with a 2 mm crochet hook)
Rnd 1: start 6 sc in a magic ring [6]
Rnd 2 – 4: sc in all 6 st [6]
Rnd 5: inc in all 6 st [12]
Rnd 6: (sc in next st, inc in next st) repeat 6 times [18]
Rnd 7: (sc in next 2 st, inc in next st) repeat 6 times [24]
Rnd 8: (slst in next st, ch 3 (picture 33), start in second ch from hook, slst in this ch, sc in next ch, slst in

next st) repeat 12 times (picture 34).

Fasten off, leaving a long tail for sewing.

Put the petal parts on top of each other and sew them together, using the leftover yarn tail. Sew the green flower heart to the center of the white flower (picture 35). Sew the flower on top of the hair.

ARM VINE (in green yarn)

Leave a long starting yarn tail. Ch 30. Fasten off, leaving a long tail for sewing.

Take a yarn tail on your sewing needle. Insert the needle into the wrist (picture 36) and come out on the other side of the arm. Roll the chain around the arm (picture 37). Take the other yarn tail on your sewing needle. Insert the needle at the end of the vine and come back out again in the wrist (picture 38). Tie the yarn tails together and hide the yarn ends.

Alwyn
THE WIZARD

A DESIGN BY BLUE SPARROW HANDMADE (BIANCA FLATMAN)

As a child, Alwyn first discovered he had magical talent when he accidentally enlarged his family cat by threefold, with no one able to shrink the cat down for at least 2 hours. He studied vigorously before enrolling in the wizarding school as a teenager. He later roamed the world learning about folklore, ancient spells, fantastical creatures and complex magic.

Skill level: ★★
Size: 9.5 in / 24 cm tall when made with the indicated yarn

Amigurumi gallery: Scan or visit
www.amigurumi.com/4408
to share pictures and find inspiration.

YOU WILL NEED:

Fingering weight yarn
- skin color of your choice
- blue
- light blue
- dark brown
- light brown
- light gray
- white
- cream

Fingering weight yarn
- gold

Size B-1 / 2.5 mm crochet hook
Safety eyes (7 mm)
Stitch markers
Yarn needle
Pins
Fiberfill
Optional: light pink makeup blush

HEAD (in skin color yarn)

Rnd 1: start 6 sc in a magic ring [6]
Rnd 2: inc in all 6 st [12]
Rnd 3: (sc in next st, inc in next st) repeat 6 times [18]
Rnd 4: (sc in next 2 st, inc in next st) repeat 6 times [24]
Rnd 5: (sc in next 3 st, inc in next st) repeat 6 times [30]
Rnd 6: (sc in next 4 st, inc in next st) repeat 6 times [36]
Rnd 7: (sc in next 5 st, inc in next st) repeat 6 times [42]
Rnd 8: (sc in next 6 st, inc in next st) repeat 6 times [48]
Rnd 9: (sc in next 7 st, inc in next st) repeat 6 times [54]
Rnd 10 – 12: sc in all 54 st [54]
Rnd 13: (sc in next 8 st, inc in next st) repeat 6 times [60]
Rnd 14 – 25: sc in all 60 st [60]
Insert the safety eyes between rounds 19 and 20, with an interspace of 10 stitches. Stuff the head with fiberfill and continue stuffing as you go.
Rnd 26: (sc in next 8 st, dec) repeat 6 times [54]
Rnd 27: (sc in next 7 st, dec) repeat 6 times [48]
Rnd 28: (sc in next 6 st, dec) repeat 6 times [42]
Rnd 29: (sc in next 5 st, dec) repeat 6 times [36]
Rnd 30: (sc in next 4 st, dec) repeat 6 times [30]
Rnd 31: (sc in next 3 st, dec) repeat 6 times [24]
Fasten off and weave in the yarn ends.

EYEBROW (make 2, in white yarn)

Ch 10. Crochet in rows.
Row 1: start in third ch from hook, hdc in next 7 st, sc in next st [8]
Fasten off, leaving a long tail for sewing.

NOSE (in skin color yarn)

Rnd 1: start 6 sc in a magic ring [6]
Rnd 2: inc in all 6 st [12]
Rnd 3: sc in all 12 st [12]
Fasten off, leaving a long tail for sewing. The nose doesn't need to be stuffed.

MUSTACHE (make 2 parts, in white yarn)

Rnd 1: start 6 sc in a magic ring [6]
Rnd 2: inc in all 6 st [12]
Rnd 3 – 6: sc in all 12 st [12]
Rnd 7: (sc in next st, dec) repeat 4 times [8]
Rnd 8 – 10: sc in all 8 st [8]
Rnd 11: inc in next 3 st, sc in next st, dec 2 times [9]
Rnd 12 – 13: sc in all 9 st [9]
The mustache pieces don't need to be stuffed. Flatten the opening of the mustache with the last stitch on the side and work the next round through both layers to close.
Rnd 14: sc in next 4 st [4]
Fasten off, leaving a long tail for sewing.

BEARD (in white yarn)

Rnd 1: start 6 sc in a magic ring [6]
Rnd 2: (sc in next st, inc in next st) repeat 3 times [9]
Rnd 3 – 4: sc in all 9 st [9]

Rnd 12: sc in all 21 st [21]
Rnd 13: (sc in next 6 st, inc in next st) repeat 3 times [24]
Rnd 14: (sc in next 7 st, inc in next st) repeat 3 times [27]
Rnd 15: (sc in next 8 st, inc in next st) repeat 3 times [30]
Rnd 16: sc in all 30 st [30]
Rnd 17: (sc in next 4 st, inc in next st) repeat 6 times [36]
Rnd 18: (sc in next 5 st, inc in next st) repeat 6 times [42]
Rnd 19: (sc in next 6 st, inc in next st) repeat 6 times [48]
Rnd 20: (sc in next 7 st, inc in next st) repeat 6 times [54]
Rnd 21 – 29: sc in all 54 st [54]
Rnd 30: sc in next 14 st [14] Leave the remaining stitches unworked.
Note: Check to see if the position of the bump in round 11 is positioned at the side. Add or remove stitches in round 30 if necessary.
The beard doesn't need to be stuffed. Flatten the opening of the beard with the last stitch on the side and work the next round through both layers to close.
Rnd 31: sc in next 27 st [27]
Fasten off, leaving a long tail for sewing.

HAIR (in cream yarn)
Rnd 1: start 6 sc in a magic ring [6]
Rnd 2: inc in all 6 st [12]
Rnd 3: (sc in next st, inc in next st) repeat 6 times [18]
Rnd 4: (sc in next 2 st, inc in next st) repeat 6 times [24]
Rnd 5: (sc in next 3 st, inc in next st) repeat 6 times [30]
Rnd 6: (sc in next 4 st, inc in next st) repeat 6 times [36]
Rnd 7: (sc in next 5 st, inc in next st) repeat 6 times [42]
Rnd 8: (sc in next 6 st, inc in next st) repeat 6 times [48]
Rnd 9: (sc in next 7 st, inc in next st) repeat 6 times [54]
Rnd 10: (sc in next 8 st, inc in next st) repeat 6 times [60]
Rnd 11 – 20: sc in all 60 st [60]
Rnd 21: (sc in next st, ch 8, slst in same st) repeat 19 times, (sc in next st, ch 16, slst in same st) repeat 41 times [60 hair locks] (picture 1)
Fasten off, leaving a long tail for sewing.

Rnd 5: (sc in next 2 st, inc in next st) repeat 3 times [12]
Rnd 6: sc in all 12 st [12]
Rnd 7: (sc in next 3 st, inc in next st) repeat 3 times [15]
Rnd 8: (sc in next 4 st, inc in next st) repeat 3 times [18]
Rnd 9: (sc in next 5 st, inc in next st) repeat 3 times [21]
Rnd 10: sc in all 21 st [21]
Rnd 11: (sc in next st, dec) repeat 3 times, sc in next 4 st, (inc in next st, sc in next st) repeat 3 times, sc in next 2 st [21]

LEG (make 2, start in dark brown yarn)

Leg 1

Rnd 1: start 7 sc in a magic ring [7]

Rnd 2: inc in all 7 st [14]

Rnd 3: (sc in next st, inc in next st) repeat 7 times [21]

Rnd 4: sc in next 8 st, inc in next st, hdc in next 3 st, inc in next st, sc in next 8 st [23]

Rnd 5: BLO sc in all 23 st [23]

Rnd 6: sc in all 23 st [23]

Rnd 7: sc in next 10 st, (dec, sc in next st) repeat 3 times, sc in next 4 st [20]

Rnd 8: sc in next 10 st, dec 2 times, sc in next 6 st [18]

Rnd 9: sc in next 9 st, dec 2 times, sc in next 5 st [16]

Rnd 10: BLO sc in all 16 st [16]

Change to light brown yarn. Stuff the leg with fiberfill and continue stuffing as you go.

Rnd 11 – 14: sc in all 16 st [16]

Rnd 15: (sc in next 3 st, inc in next st) repeat 4 times [20]

Rnd 16: (sc in next 4 st, inc in next st) repeat 4 times [24]

Rnd 17 – 18: sc in all 24 st [24]

Rnd 19: (sc in next 5 st, inc in next st) repeat 4 times [28]

Rnd 20: (sc in next 6 st, inc in next st) repeat 4 times [32]

Rnd 21: sc in all 32 st [32]

Fasten off and weave in the yarn end. Mark the 23rd stitch of round 21 with a stitch marker (picture 2).

Note: Check to see if the last stitch is positioned on the inside of the leg, with the foot pointing slightly inward. Add or remove stitches in round 21 if necessary.

Hold the leg upside down and pull up a loop of dark brown yarn in the first remaining front loop of round 4.

Decorative round 1: FLO sc in all 23 st [23]

Fasten off and weave in the yarn end.

Hold the leg upright and pull up a loop of dark brown yarn in the first remaining front loop of round 9.

Decorative round 2: FLO slst in all 16 st [16]

Fasten off and weave in the yarn end.

Leg 2

Rnd 1 – 20: repeat the pattern for leg 1.

Rnd 21: sc in next 27 st [27] Leave the remaining stitches unworked.

Don't fasten off, but pause and put aside the light brown yarn as you make the decorative rounds.

Hold the leg upside down and pull up a loop of dark brown yarn in the first remaining front loop of round 4.

Decorative round 1: FLO sc in next 23 st [23]

Fasten off and weave in the yarn end.

Hold the leg upright and pull up a loop of dark brown yarn in the first remaining front loop of round 9.

Decorative round 2: FLO slst in next 16 st [16]

Fasten off and weave in the yarn end. In the next round we'll join both legs to make the body.

BODY

Rnd 22: insert your hook into the next stitch of leg 2 and the marked stitch of leg 1 (picture 3), and join both legs with a sc. Sc in the same stitch of leg 1 only (this will help to avoid holes between the legs), sc in next 30 st, insert your hook into the next st of leg 1 and the next available stitch of leg 2 (picture 4), join both legs with a sc, sc in the same stitch of leg 2 only, sc in next 30 st [64] (picture 5)

Rnd 23: (sc in next 15 st, inc in next st) repeat 4 times [68]

Rnd 24 – 33: sc in all 68 st [68]

Change to light gray yarn.

Rnd 34: BLO sc in all 68 st [68]

Rnd 35: sc in all 68 st [68]

Rnd 36: (sc in next 15 st, dec) repeat 4 times [64]

Rnd 37: sc in all 64 st [64]

Rnd 38: (sc in next 14 st, dec) repeat 4 times [60]

Rnd 39: sc in all 60 st [60]

Rnd 40: (sc in next 13 st, dec) repeat 4 times [56]

Rnd 41 – 43: sc in all 56 st [56]

Rnd 44: (sc in next 12 st, dec) repeat 4 times [52]

Rnd 45 – 46: sc in all 52 st [52]

Rnd 47: (sc in next 11 st, dec) repeat 4 times [48]

Rnd 48: (sc in next 10 st, dec) repeat 4 times [44]

Rnd 49: (sc in next 9 st, dec) repeat 4 times [40]

Rnd 50: (sc in next 8 st, dec) repeat 4 times [36]

Stuff the body with fiberfill and continue stuffing as you go.

Rnd 51: (sc in next 7 st, dec) repeat 4 times [32]

Rnd 52: (sc in next 6 st, dec) repeat 4 times [28]

Rnd 53: (sc in next 5 st, dec) repeat 4 times [24]

Fasten off, leaving a long tail for sewing. Hold the body upright and pull up a loop of light brown yarn in the first remaining front loop of round 33.

Decorative round: FLO slst in all 68 st [68] (picture 6)

Fasten off and weave in the yarn end.

ASSEMBLY OF THE FACE

- Position the beard between rounds 21 and 22 of the head, centered below the eyes (picture 7). Sew round 31 of the beard to the head, leaving the remainder of the beard free.
- Position the nose centered between the eyes and slightly on top of the beard. Sew the nose to the head, with the top of the nose sewn between rounds 18 and 19.
- Sew round 14 of the mustache pieces to the sides of the nose, leaving the remainder of the mustache free. The mustache will sit partially on top of the beard (picture 8).
- Position and sew the eyebrows above each eye at a slight angle, across rounds 14 to 19 of the head (picture 9).
- Place the hair onto the head, ensuring the shorter hair locks are at the front. Sew the hair piece on with a few random stitches.
- Optionally, add a bit of makeup blush beside each eye.

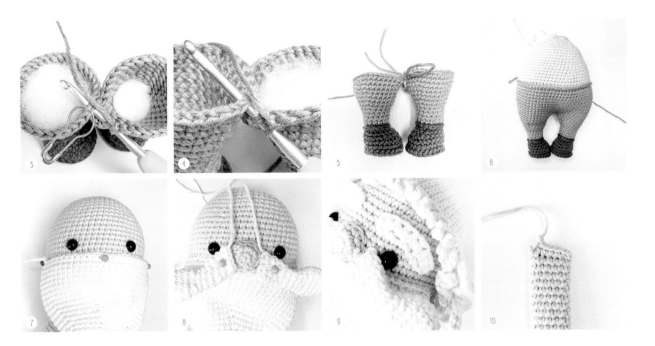

• Sew the head to the body. Add more fiberfill to the neck before closing the seam.

ARM (make 2, start in skin color yarn)
Rnd 1: start 6 sc in a magic ring [6]
Rnd 2: inc in all 6 st [12]
Rnd 3: (sc in next 2 st, inc in next st) repeat 4 times [16]
Rnd 4 – 5: sc in all 16 st [16]
Rnd 6 right arm: sc in next 4 st, 4-dc-bobble in next st, sc in next 11 st [16]
Rnd 6 left arm: sc in next 11 st, 4-dc-bobble in next st, sc in next 4 st [16]
Rnd 7: (sc in next 2 st, dec) repeat 4 times [12]
Rnd 8 – 9: sc in all 12 st [12]
Change to light gray yarn.
Rnd 10: sc in all 12 st [12]
Rnd 11: BLO sc in all 12 st [12]
Stuff rounds 1-10 with fiberfill but don't stuff the next rounds.

Rnd 12 – 22: sc in all 12 st [12]
Rnd 23: sc in next 8 st [8] Leave the remaining stitches unworked.
Flatten the opening of the arm with the last stitch on the side and work the next round through both layers to close.
Rnd 24: sc in all 6 st [6] (picture 10)
Fasten off, leaving a long tail for sewing. Hold the arm upright and pull up a loop of light gray yarn in the first remaining front loop of round 10.
Decorative round: FLO slst in all 12 st [12]
Fasten off and weave in the yarn end. Sew the arms to the sides of the body between rounds 50 and 51, with an interspace of 10 stitches between the arms at the front.

HAT (in light blue yarn)
Rnd 1: start 6 sc in a magic ring [6]
Rnd 2: (sc in next st, inc in next st) repeat 3 times [9]

Rnd 3: sc in all 9 st [9]

Rnd 4: (sc in next 2 st, inc in next st) repeat 3 times [12]

Rnd 5: sc in all 12 st [12]

Rnd 6: (sc in next 3 st, inc in next st) repeat 3 times [15]

Rnd 7: (sc in next st, dec) repeat 2 times, sc in next 2 st, inc in next 4 st, sc in next 3 st [17]

Rnd 8: sc in all 17 st [17]

Rnd 9: sc in next 8 st, inc in next st, sc in next 8 st [18]

Rnd 10: (sc in next 2 st, inc in next st) repeat 6 times [24]

Rnd 11: sc in all 24 st [24]

Rnd 12: (inc in next st, sc in next st) repeat 3 times, sc in next 3 st, dec 3 times, sc in next 9 st [24]

Rnd 13: sc in all 24 st [24]

Rnd 14: (sc in next 3 st, inc in next st) repeat 6 times [30]

Rnd 15: (sc in next 4 st, inc in next st) repeat 6 times [36]

Rnd 16: (sc in next 5 st, inc in next st) repeat 6 times [42]

Rnd 17: sc in all 42 st [42]

Rnd 18: (sc in next 6 st, inc in next st) repeat 6 times [48]

Rnd 19: sc in all 48 st [48]

Rnd 20: (sc in next 7 st, inc in next st) repeat 6 times [54]

Rnd 21: sc in all 54 st [54]

Rnd 22: (sc in next 8 st, inc in next st) repeat 6 times [60]

Rnd 23: sc in all 60 st [60]

Rnd 24: (sc in next 9 st, inc in next st) repeat 6 times [66]

Rnd 25 − 27: sc in all 66 st [66]

Rnd 28: (sc in next 10 st, inc in next st) repeat 6 times [72]

Rnd 29 − 30: sc in all 72 st [72]

Rnd 31: FLO sc in all 72 st [72]

Rnd 32: (sc in next 11 st, inc in next st) repeat 6 times [78]

Rnd 33: sc in all 78 st [78]

Rnd 34: (sc in next 12 st, inc in next st) repeat 6 times [84]

Rnd 35 − 36: sc in all 84 st [84]

Fasten off and weave in the yarn end. Place the hat onto the head.

COAT (start in blue yarn)

Ch 41. Crochet in rows.

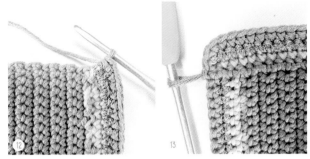

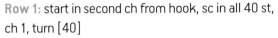

Row 1: start in second ch from hook, sc in all 40 st, ch 1, turn [40]

Row 2: (inc in next st, sc in next 9 st) repeat 3 times, sc in next 9 st, inc in next st, ch 1, turn [44]

Row 3: sc in next 6 st, ch 8, skip next 8 st, sc in next 16 st, ch 8, skip next 8 st, sc in next 6 st, ch 1, turn [28 + 16 ch]

Row 4: sc in next 6 st, sc in next 8 ch, sc in next 16 st, sc in next 8 ch, sc in next 6 st, ch 1, turn [44] (picture 11)

Row 5: (sc in next 10 st, inc in next st) repeat 3 times, sc in next 11 st, ch 1, turn [47]

Row 6: (sc in next 11 st, inc in next st) repeat 3 times, sc in next 11 st, ch 1, turn [50]

Row 7: sc in next 9 st, inc in next st, sc in next 9 st, inc in next 2 st, sc in next 18 st, inc in next 2 st, sc in next 9 st, ch 1, turn [55]

Row 8: sc in all 55 st, ch 1, turn [55]

Row 9: sc in next 10 st, inc in next st, sc in next 10 st, inc in next 2 st, sc in next 20 st, inc in next 2 st, sc in next 10 st, ch 1, turn [60]

Row 10: sc in next 11 st, inc in next st, sc in next 11 st, inc in next 2 st, sc in next 22 st, inc in next 2 st, sc in next 11 st, ch 1, turn [65]

Row 11: sc in all 65 st, ch 1, turn [65]

Row 12: sc in next 12 st, inc in next st, sc in next 12 st, inc in next 2 st, sc in next 24 st, inc in next 2 st, sc in next 12 st, ch 1, turn [70]

Row 13: sc in next 13 st, inc in next st, sc in next 13 st, inc in next 2 st, sc in next 26 st, inc in next 2 st, sc in next 13 st, ch 1, turn [75]

Row 14 – 33: sc in all 75 st, ch 1, turn [75]

Work the next row with alternating colors. You can use the jacquard technique. The color changes are indicated in italics.

Row 34: ((*blue*) sc in next 2 st, (*light gray*) sc in next 2 st) repeat 18 times, (*blue*) sc in next 2 st, (*light gray*) sc in next st, ch 1, turn [75]

Continue in light gray yarn.

Row 35: sc in all 75 st, ch 1, turn [75]

Change to golden yarn.

Row 36: sc in all 75 st, ch 1, turn [75]

Change to blue yarn.

Row 37: sc in all 75 st [75]

Fasten off and weave in the yarn end.

COAT BORDER (start in blue yarn)

When working the right-hand side of the coat, you will have the right side facing you. When working the left-hand side of the coat, you will have the wrong side facing you.

With the coat on its side, pull up a loop of blue yarn in the top right-hand corner, in row 37 of the coat. Work the first stitch of the next row in this stitch (picture 12).

Row 1: sc in all 36 row-ends along one side of the coat, change to light gray yarn, ch 1, turn [36]

Row 2: sc in all 36 st, change to golden yarn, ch 1, turn [36]

Row 3: sc in all 36 st, change to blue yarn, ch 1, turn [36]
Row 4: sc in all 36 st, do not ch 1 and turn, instead sc in next 2 row-ends along the bottom edge, back to where you started [38] (picture 13)
Fasten off and weave in the yarn end. Repeat this for the opposite side.

SLEEVE (make 2, start in blue yarn)
With the right side of the coat facing you, pull up a loop of blue yarn in the bottom left stitch of the armhole, ch 1 (picture 14). Work the next round in 18 stitches (8 skipped stiches, 8 stitches on the chain, and 2 corner spaces between the skipped stitches and the chain stitches).
Rnd 1: (inc in next st, sc in next 2 st) repeat 6 times [24]
Rnd 2 – 4: sc in all 24 st [24]
Rnd 5: (inc in next st, sc in next 3 st) repeat 6 times [30]
Rnd 6 – 14: sc in all 30 st [30]
Change to light gray yarn.
Rnd 15: sc in all 30 st [30]
Change to golden yarn.
Rnd 16: sc in all 30 st [30]
Change to blue yarn.
Rnd 17: sc in all 30 st [30]
Fasten off and weave in the yarn end (picture 15).

Fold the edge of each sleeve up, to create the cuff look. Put the coat on, folding the collar flaps of the coat down.

COAT BELT (in dark brown yarn)

Ch 100 and fasten off. Trim the starting and ending yarn tails, they should be 0.4 in / 1 cm long.
Tie the coat belt around the waist of the wizard and make a bow.

WIZARD STAFF (in dark brown yarn)

Rnd 1: start 6 sc in a magic ring [6]
Rnd 2: (sc in next st, inc in next st) repeat 3 times [9]
Rnd 3 – 4: sc in all 9 st [9]
Rnd 5: (sc in next 2 st, inc in next st) repeat 3 times [12]
Rnd 6: (sc in next st, inc in next st) repeat 6 times [18]
Rnd 7: (sc in next 2 st, inc in next st) repeat 6 times [24]
Rnd 8 – 10: sc in all 24 st [24]
Rnd 11: (sc in next 2 st, dec) repeat 6 times [18]
Rnd 12: (sc in next st, dec) repeat 6 times [12]
Rnd 13 – 14: inc in next st, sc in next 5 st, dec, sc in next 4 st [12]
Stuff the staff with fiberfill and continue stuffing as you go.
Rnd 15: sc in all 12 st [12]
Rnd 16: inc in next st, sc in next 5 st, dec, sc in next 4 st [12]
Rnd 17: inc in next 2 st, sc in next 2 st, dec 2 times, sc in next 4 st [12]
Rnd 18: sc in all 12 st [12]
Rnd 19 – 20: sc in next st, dec 2 times, sc in next 2 st, inc in next 2 st, sc in next 3 st [12]
Rnd 21 – 22: sc in all 12 st [12]
Rnd 23: sc in next 2 st, inc in next st, sc in next 4 st, dec, sc in next 3 st [12]
Rnd 24 – 25: sc in all 12 st [12]
Rnd 26: sc in next 2 st, inc in next st, sc in next 4 st, dec, sc in next 3 st [12]
Rnd 27 – 28: sc in all 12 st [12]
Rnd 29 – 34: sc in next 2 st, inc in next st, sc in next 4 st, dec, sc in next 3 st [12]
Rnd 35 – 44: sc in all 12 st [12]
Rnd 45: (sc in next 2 st, dec) repeat 3 times [9]
Rnd 46 – 58: sc in all 9 st [9]
Rnd 59: sc in next st, dec 4 times [5]
Fasten off, leaving a yarn tail. Using your needle, weave the yarn tail through the front loop of each remaining stitch and pull it tight to close. Weave in the yarn end.
Pull up a loop of dark brown yarn in a stitch between rounds 22 and 23 (picture 16).
Handle: ch 15 (or any length you require to fit around the hand of the wizard), slst back into the same stitch you started in [15] (picture 17)
Fasten off and weave in the yarn end. Position one of the arms through the handle of the staff.

THE SELKIE
Morgana

A DESIGN BY AMOUR FOU (CARLA MITRANI)

Morgana the Selkie lives near the Isle of Skye in Scotland and sometimes hides her sealskin in a cave so she can sneak into the towns at night. She dreams of attending one of the festivals, mingling with the locals and even be asked to dance with a sweet boy. Have a shot of whiskey? Well, maybe she'll have a sip. But first, of course, she must learn how to conceal that shiny mint green hair of hers.

Skill level: ★ ★
Size: 11" / 28 cm tall when made with the indicated yarn

Amigurumi gallery: Scan or visit www.amigurumi.com/4409 to share pictures and find inspiration.

YOU WILL NEED:
Fingering weight yarn
- skin color of your choice
  white
- mint
- light pink (leftover)

Light worsted weight yarn
- teal
- black (leftover)

Sizes 2 mm and 2.5 mm crochet hooks
2 pairs of safety eyes (6 mm and 8 mm)
Yarn needle
Stitch markers
2 pearl beads (Ø 5 mm)
Fiberfill

Note: Use a 2 mm crochet hook, unless the pattern states otherwise.

LEG (make 2, start in skin color yarn)
Rnd 1: start 6 sc in a magic ring [6]
Rnd 2 – 3: sc in all 6 st [6]
Rnd 4: (sc in next 2 st, inc in next st) repeat 2 times [8]
Rnd 5 – 6: sc in all 8 st [8]
Stuff the leg with fiberfill and continue stuffing as you go.
Rnd 7: (sc in next 3 st, inc in next st) repeat 2 times [10]
Rnd 8 – 9: sc in all 10 st [10]
Rnd 10: (sc in next 4 st, inc in next st) repeat 2 times [12]
Rnd 11 – 13: sc in all 12 st [12]
Rnd 14: (sc in next 5 st, inc in next st) repeat 2 times [14]
Rnd 15 – 21: sc in all 14 st [14]
Change to white yarn.
Rnd 22: BLO sc in all 14 st [14]
Fasten off on the first leg and weave in the yarn end.
Don't fasten off on the second leg. In the next round we'll join both legs to make the body.

BODY
Rnd 23: sc in next 3 st, ch 2 (picture 1), sc in next st on the first leg to join, sc in next 13 st on the first leg, sc in next 2 ch, sc in next 14 st on the second leg, sc in the opposite side of next 2 ch [32]
Rnd 24: (sc in next 7 st, inc in next st) repeat 4 times [36]
Rnd 25 – 29: sc in all 36 st [36]
Change to skin color yarn.
Rnd 30: BLO sc in all 36 st [36]
Rnd 31: (sc in next 4 st, dec) repeat 6 times [30]
Rnd 32 – 33: sc in all 30 st [30]
Rnd 34: (sc in next 3 st, dec) repeat 6 times [24]
Stuff the body with fiberfill and continue stuffing as you go.
Rnd 35 – 37: sc in all 24 st [24]
Rnd 38: (sc in next 2 st, dec) repeat 6 times [18]
Rnd 39: sc in all 18 st [18]

Change to white yarn.
Rnd 40: sc in all 18 st [18]
Change to skin color yarn.
Rnd 41: BLO sc in all 18 st [18]
Rnd 42: sc in all 18 st [18]
Rnd 43: (sc in next st, dec) repeat 6 times [12]
Rnd 44 – 47: sc in all 12 st [12]
Rnd 48: BLO sc in all 12 st [12]
Rnd 49 – 50: sc in all 12 st [12]
Stuff the neck firmly with fiberfill.
Rnd 51: dec 6 times [6]
Fasten off and weave in the yarn end.

WHITE DRESS (in white yarn)
Hold the body upside down and pull up a loop of white
yarn in one of the leftover front loops of round 40,
on the back, where the color changes are (picture 2).
Rnd 1: FLO sc in all 18 st [18]
Rnd 2: sc in next st, inc in next st, (sc in next 2 st,
inc in next st) repeat 5 times, sc in next st [24]

Rnd 3 – 4: sc in all 24 st [24]
Rnd 5: (sc in next 3 st, inc in next st) repeat 6 times [30]
Rnd 6 – 7: sc in all 30 st [30]
Rnd 8: sc in next 2 st, inc in next st, (sc in next 4 st,
inc in next st) repeat 5 times, sc in next 2 st [36]
Rnd 9 – 10: sc in all 36 st [36]
Rnd 11: (sc in next 5 st, inc in next st) repeat 6 times [42]
Rnd 12 – 20: sc in all 42 st [42]
Rnd 21: (slst in next st, sc in next st, hdc in next st, dc in
next st, hdc in next st, sc in next st) repeat 7 times [42]
Slst in first st. Fasten off and weave in the yarn end.

HEAD (in skin color yarn)
Hold the body upright and pull up a loop of skin color
yarn in one of the leftover front loops of round 47 of
the neck, on the back, where the color changes are
(picture 3).
Rnd 1: FLO inc in all 12 st [24]
Rnd 2: (sc in next st, inc in next st) repeat 12 times [36]
Rnd 3: (sc in next 5 st, inc in next st) repeat 6 times [42]

Rnd 4: sc in next 3 st, inc in next st, (sc in next 6 st, inc in next st) repeat 5 times, sc in next 3 st [48]
Rnd 5 – 6: sc in all 48 st [48]
Rnd 7: sc in next 28 st, 5-dc-bobble in next st (to form the nose, it should be centered relative to the legs) (pictures 4-5), sc in next 19 st [48]
Note: If you end up with the nose protruding from the wrong side of the fabric (picture 6), you can just push it outward (picture 7).
Rnd 8 – 18: sc in all 48 st [48]
Insert the safety eyes between rounds 8 and 9, with an interspace of 10 stitches. Embroider cheeks with light pink yarn.
Rnd 19: sc in next 3 st, dec, (sc in next 6 st, dec) repeat 5 times, sc in next 3 st [42]
Stuff the head with fiberfill and continue stuffing as you go.
Rnd 20: (sc in next 5 st, dec) repeat 6 times [36]
Rnd 21: sc in next 2 st, dec, (sc in next 4 st, dec) repeat 5 times, sc in next 2 st [30]
Rnd 22: (sc in next 3 st, dec) repeat 6 times [24]
Rnd 23: sc in next st, dec, (sc in next 2 st, dec) repeat 5 times, sc in next st [18]
Rnd 24: (sc in next st, dec) repeat 6 times [12]
Rnd 25: dec 6 times [6]
Fasten off and weave in the yarn end.

ARM (make 2, in skin color yarn)
Rnd 1: start 4 sc in a magic ring [4]
Rnd 2: inc in all 4 st [8]
Rnd 3 – 24: sc in all 8 st [8]
The arm doesn't need to be stuffed. Flatten the opening of the arm with the last stitch on the side and work the next round through both layers to close.
Rnd 25: sc in all 4 st [4]
Fasten off, leaving a long tail for sewing. Sew the arms on both sides of the body, between rounds 44 and 45.

STRAP OF THE DRESS (in white yarn)
Leave a long starting yarn tail, ch 18. Fasten off, leaving a long tail for sewing. Wrap the strap around the neck and sew it in the middle of the chest using both yarn tails.

HAIR (in mint yarn)
Rnd 1: start 6 sc in a magic ring [6]
Rnd 2: inc in all 6 st [12]
Rnd 3: (sc in next st, inc in next st) repeat 6 times [18]
Rnd 4: sc in next st, inc in next st, (sc in next 2 st, inc in next st) repeat 5 times, sc in next st [24]
Rnd 5: (sc in next 3 st, inc in next st) repeat 6 times [30]
Rnd 6: sc in next 2 st, inc in next st, (sc in next 4 st, inc in next st) repeat 5 times, sc in next 2 st [36]
Rnd 7: (sc in next 5 st, inc in next st) repeat 6 times [42]
Rnd 8: sc in next 3 st, inc in next st, (sc in next 6 st, inc in next st) repeat 5 times, sc in next 3 st [48]
Rnd 9: (sc in next 23 st, inc in next st) repeat 2 times [50]
Rnd 10 – 17: sc in all 50 st [50]
Rnd 18: slst in next st, ch 55, start in second ch from hook, sc in all 54 ch, sc in next 2 st, (ch 7 (picture 8), start in second ch from hook, sc in all 6 ch, sc in next 2 st) repeat 2 times, ch 55, start in second ch from hook, sc in all 54 ch, slst in next st, sc in next 21 st, (ch 35, start in second ch from hook, sc in all 34 ch, slst in next st) repeat 2 times. Leave the remaining stitches unworked.
Fasten off, leaving a long tail for sewing. The long locks will curve naturally (and if they don't, curl them with your fingers). Sew the hair piece to the head and sew the two short hairlocks to the forehead with a few stitches (picture 9). Then part the two long hairlocks to the sides and loosely tie them with the medium hair-locks at the back to create a ponytail.

SEALSKIN

Seal tail (in teal yarn, with a 2.5 mm crochet hook)
Rnd 1: start 6 sc in a magic ring [6]
Rnd 2: inc in all 6 st [12]
Rnd 3 – 4: sc in all 12 st [12]
Rnd 5: (sc in next st, inc in next st) repeat 6 times [18]
Rnd 6 – 7: sc in all 18 st [18]
Rnd 8: sc in next st, inc in next st, (sc in next 2 st, inc in next st) repeat 5 times, sc in next st [24]
Rnd 9 – 10: sc in all 24 st [24]
Rnd 11: (inc in next st, sc in next 11 st) repeat 2 times [26]
Rnd 12 – 13: sc in all 26 st [26]
Rnd 14: (sc in next 6 st, inc in next st, sc in next 6 st) repeat 2 times [28]
Rnd 15 – 16: sc in all 28 st [28]
Rnd 17: (inc in next st, sc in next 13 st) repeat 2 times [30]
Rnd 18 – 19: sc in all 30 st [30]
Rnd 20: (sc in next 7 st, inc in next st, sc in next 7 st) repeat 2 times [32]
Rnd 21 – 22: sc in all 32 st [32]
Rnd 23: (inc in next st, sc in next 15 st) repeat 2 times [34]
Rnd 24 – 25: sc in all 34 st [34]
Rnd 26: (sc in next 8 st, inc in next st, sc in next 8 st) repeat 2 times [36]

Rnd 27 – 28: sc in all 36 st [36]
Note: Try the seal tail on and add a couple of rounds if necessary.
Fasten off and weave in the yarn end.

Fin (make 2, in teal yarn, with a 2.5 mm crochet hook)
Rnd 1: start 6 sc in a magic ring [6]
Rnd 2: sc in all 6 st [6]
Rnd 3: inc in all 6 st [12]
Rnd 4 – 5: sc in all 12 st [12]
Rnd 6: (sc in next st, inc in next st) repeat 6 times [18]
Rnd 7 – 10: sc in all 18 st [18]
Rnd 11: (sc in next st, dec) repeat 6 times [12]
Rnd 12 – 13: sc in all 12 st [12]
Rnd 14: dec 6 times [6]
Fasten off, leaving a long tail for sewing. The fin doesn't need to be stuffed. Sew both fins to the tip of the tail and weave in the yarn ends.

Hood (in teal yarn, with a 2.5 mm crochet hook)
Rnd 1: start 6 sc in a magic ring [6]
Rnd 2: inc in all 6 st [12]
Rnd 3: (sc in next st, inc in next st) repeat 6 times [18]
Rnd 4: sc in next st, inc in next st, (sc in next 2 st, inc in next st) repeat 5 times, sc in next st [24]
Rnd 5: (sc in next 3 st, inc in next st) repeat 6 times [30]
Rnd 6: sc in next 2 st, inc in next st, (sc in next 4 st, inc in next st) repeat 5 times, sc in next 2 st [36]

Rnd 7: (sc in next 5 st, inc in next st) repeat 6 times [42]

Rnd 8: sc in next 3 st, inc in next st, (sc in next 6 st, inc in next st) repeat 5 times, sc in next 3 st [48]

Rnd 9 – 17: sc in all 48 st [48]

Don't fasten off. Continue making the cape. Crochet in rows.

Row 1: ch 18, start in third ch from hook, dc in first 5 ch, hdc in next 5 ch, sc in next 3 ch, slst in last 2 ch (picture 10), slst in next st on the hood, turn.

Row 2: work this row in BLO: slst in first 2 st, sc in next 3 st, hdc in next 5 st, dc in last 5 st (picture 11), ch 3, turn.

Row 3: work this row in BLO: dc in next 5 st, hdc in next 5 st, sc in next 3 st, slst in next 2 st, slst in next st on the hood, turn.

Row 4 – 25: repeat rows 2 and 3 alternatively. The last row you make should repeat the pattern of row 3, to finish on the hood. Then ch 25 to create the first strap. Fasten off.

Pull up a loop of teal yarn in the corner stitch on the other side of the cape and make a slst (picture 12). Ch 25 to create the second strap. Add a pearl bead to the end of each strap and make a knot to secure the bead in place.

Muzzle (in teal yarn, with a 2.5 mm crochet hook)

Rnd 1: start 6 sc in a magic ring [6]

Rnd 2: inc in all 6 st [12]

Rnd 3: (sc in next st, inc in next st) repeat 6 times [18]

Rnd 4 – 5: sc in all 18 st [18]

Fasten off, leaving a long tail for sewing. Stuff the muzzle lightly with fiberfill and sew it to rounds 9-15 of the hood. Embroider the nose on rounds 1-2 of the muzzle with black yarn.

Insert the safety eyes at 2 stitches from the muzzle, between rounds 12 and 13 of the hood. You can also choose to embroider the eyes with black yarn. Embroider the cheeks with light pink yarn.

Sofia

FROM UNICORN WONDERLAND

A DESIGN BY GREEN FROG CROCHET (THUY ANH)

Sofia is a princess from the Unicorn Wonderland. She loves caring for her unicorns and sometimes dresses up as one of them, to feel more connected to her wondrous friends. Her favorite outfit consists of a rainbow dress, shiny boots and a unicorn headband to tie it all together. Oh, and everything needs a lot of glitter, of course.

Skill level: ★ ★
Size: 10 in / 25 cm tall when made with the indicated yarn

Amigurumi gallery: Scan or visit
www.amigurumi.com/4410
to share pictures and find inspiration.

YOU WILL NEED:
Fingering weight yarn
- skin color of your choice
- white
- pink
- purple
- blue

Light worsted weight yarn
- gold

Sizes B-1 / 2 mm and C-2 / 2.75 mm crochet hooks
Safety eyes (9 mm)
Dark brown embroidery thread
Sewing needle
Button (Ø 9 mm)
Fiberfill
Optional: small piece of plastic
Optional: fabric glue
Optional: pink makeup blush

Note: Use a B-1 / 2 mm crochet hook unless the pattern states otherwise.

ARM (make 2, in skin color yarn)
Rnd 1: start 6 sc in a magic ring [6]
Rnd 2: inc in all 6 st [12]
Rnd 3 – 5: sc in all 12 st [12]
Rnd 6: 4-dc-bobble in next st, sc in next 11 st [12] (picture 1)
Rnd 7: sc in next 5 st, dec 2 times, sc in next 3 st [10]
Rnd 8 – 24: sc in all 10 st [10]
Slst in next st. Fasten off and weave in the yarn end. The arms don't need to be stuffed. Mark the stitch straight above the bobble stitch (the thumb) on round 24 with a stitch marker.

EAR (make 2, in skin color yarn)
Work in rows.

Row 1: start 6 sc in a magic ring, ch 1, turn [6]
Row 2: sc in all 6 st [6]
Fasten off, leaving a long tail for sewing.

NECK TUBE (in skin color yarn)
Note: The tube will be placed inside the neck for extra strength.
Rnd 1: start 6 sc in a magic ring [6]
Rnd 2: (inc in next 2 st, sc in next st) repeat 2 times [10]
Rnd 3 – 12: sc in all 10 st [10]
Slst in next st. Fasten off and weave in the yarn end.

RIGHT LEG (in skin color yarn)
Ch. 6. Stitches are worked around both sides of the foundation chain.
Rnd 1: start in second ch from hook, sc in next 4 st, 4 sc in next st. Continue on the other side of the foundation chain, sc in next 3 st, 3 sc in next st [14]
Rnd 2: (inc in next st, sc in next 3 st, inc in next 3 st) repeat 2 times [22]
Rnd 3: sc in next 5 st, (inc in next st, sc in next st) repeat 4 times, sc in next 5 st, (inc in next st, sc in next st) repeat 2 times [28]
Rnd 4 – 5: sc in all 28 st [28]
Rnd 6: sc in next 5 st, (dec, sc in next 2 st) repeat 4 times, sc in next 7 st [24]
Rnd 7: sc in next 3 st, (dec, sc in next 2 st) repeat 4 times, sc in next 5 st [20]
Note: You can cut and insert a piece of plastic into the foot before stuffing, to strengthen and flatten the feet. Stuff the foot and leg with fiberfill and continue stuffing as you go (picture 2).
Rnd 8: sc in next 5 st, (dec, sc in next st) repeat 2 times, sc in next 5 st, dec 2 times [16]
Rnd 9: sc in next 4 st, (dec, sc in next st) repeat 2 times, sc in next 6 st [14]
Rnd 10 – 36: sc in next 14 st [14]

Slst in next st. Fasten off. Mark the middle stitch on the inside of the right leg with a stitch marker (green stitch marker in picture 3).

LEFT LEG (in skin color yarn)
Rnd 1 — 36: repeat the instructions for the right leg. Don't fasten off the left leg. The last stitch of round 36 should be in the center of the back side (pink stitch marker in picture 3). If necessary, make a few additional sc or undo a few until you reach this point. Change to white yarn.

BODY AND HEAD
In the next round, we'll join both legs together to make the body.
Rnd 37: sc in next 11 st on the left leg, ch 4 (picture 4), sc in the marked stitch on the right leg, sc in next 13 st on the right leg (picture 5), sc in next 4 ch between the legs, sc in next 3 st on the left leg [32 + 4 ch]

(picture 6)
Rnd 38: (inc in next st, sc in next 5 st) repeat 6 times [42]
Rnd 39 — 41: sc in all 42 st [42]
Rnd 42: (sc in next 5 st, dec) repeat 6 times [36] Change to skin color yarn.
Rnd 43: sc in all 36 st [36]
Rnd 44: (dec, sc in next 7 st) repeat 4 times [32]
Rnd 45: sc in all 32 st [32]
Rnd 46: (sc in next 6 st, dec) repeat 4 times [28]
Rnd 47: sc in all 28 st [28]
Rnd 48: (sc in next 4 st, dec, sc in next 8 st) repeat 2 times [26]
Rnd 49 — 53: sc in all 26 st [26]
In the next round, we'll join the arms to the body. Make sure to mirror the left and right arm (the thumb is pointing toward the body).
Rnd 54: sc in next 5 st on the body, sc in the marked stitch on the left arm, sc in next 9 st on the left arm,

sc in next 14 st on the body, sc in the marked stitch on the right arm, sc in next 9 st on the right arm, sc in next 7 st on the body [46] (picture 7)

Rnd 55: sc in next 3 st, dec 2 times, sc in next 7 st, dec 2 times, sc in next 8 st, dec 2 times, sc in next 7 st, dec 2 times, sc in next 5 st [38]

Rnd 56: sc in next 2 st, dec 2 times, sc in next 5 st, dec 2 times, sc in next 6 st, dec 2 times, sc in next 5 st, dec 2 times, sc in next 4 st [30]

Rnd 57: (sc in next 3 st, dec) repeat 6 times [24]
Stuff the body firmly with fiberfill. Don't stuff the arms.

Rnd 58: (sc in next 2 st, dec) repeat 6 times [18]

Rnd 59: (sc in next st, dec) repeat 6 times [12]

Rnd 60 – 63: sc in all 12 st [12]

Rnd 64: inc in all 12 st [24]

Rnd 65: (sc in next st, inc in next st) repeat 12 times [36]

Rnd 66: (sc in next 5 st, inc in next st) repeat 6 times [42]

Rnd 67: sc in next 3 st, inc in next st, (sc in next 6 st, inc in next st) repeat 5 times, sc in next 3 st [48]
Place the tube inside the doll's neck (picture 8), this will strengthen the neck. Stuff the tube firmly with fiberfill. The tube doesn't need to be closed. Continue to stuff the head with fiberfill as you go.

Rnd 68: (sc in next 7 st, inc in next st) repeat 6 times [54]

Rnd 69 – 85: sc in all 54 st [54]

Rnd 86: (sc in next 7 st, dec) repeat 6 times [48]

Rnd 87: (sc in next 6 st, dec) repeat 6 times [42]

Rnd 88: (sc in next 5 st, dec) repeat 6 times [36]

Rnd 89: (sc in next 4 st, dec) repeat 6 times [30]
Insert the safety eyes between rounds 74 and 75, with an interspace of 9 stitches. Embroider the eyelashes with dark brown embroidery thread before closing the washers.

Rnd 90: (sc in next 3 st, dec) repeat 6 times [24]

Rnd 91: (sc in next st, dec) repeat 8 times [16]

Rnd 92: dec 8 times [8]
Fasten off, leaving a long yarn tail. Using your yarn needle, weave the yarn tail through the front loop of each remaining stitch and pull it tight to close. Weave in the yarn end.

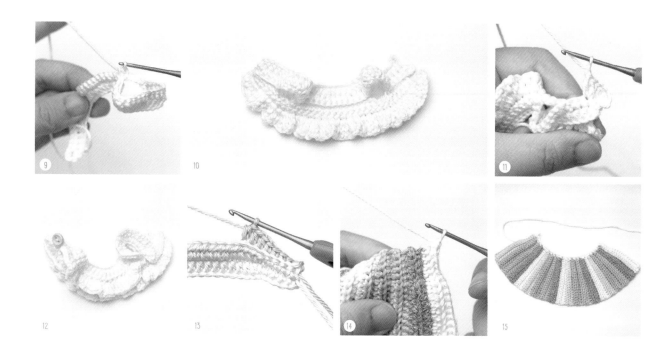

DRESS

Upper part of the dress (start in white yarn)
Ch 33. Crochet in rows.
Row 1: start in second ch from hook, hdc in next 6 st, (hdc inc in next st, hdc in next 3 st) repeat 6 times, hdc in next 2 st, ch 5, turn [38]
Row 2: start in sixth st from hook *(this creates the buttonhole)*, sc in next 5 st, inc in next st, (sc in next 6 st, inc in next st, sc in next 6 st) repeat 2 times, inc in next st, sc in next 5 st, ch 1, turn [42]
Row 3: work this row in BLO: sc in next 5 st, ch 3, skip next 10 st, inc in next st, sc in next 10 st, inc in next st, ch 3, skip next 10 st, sc in next 5 st, ch 1, turn [24 + 6 ch] (picture 9)
Row 4: sc in all 30 st, ch 1, turn [30]
Row 5: sc in all 30 st, ch 2, turn [30]
Row 6: work this row in BLO: (dc inc in next st, ch 1) repeat 29 times, dc inc in next st, ch 2.

Slst in next st. Fasten off and weave in the yarn end (picture 10). Sew a small button on row 2 of the dress, to make the dress removable.

Ruffle
Work in the leftover front loops of row 2 of the upper part of the dress. Pull up a loop of white yarn, ch 2 (picture 11).
Row 1: work this row in FLO, (dc inc in next st, ch 1) repeat 41 times, dc inc in next st, ch 2. Slst in next st. Fasten off and weave in the yarn end (picture 12).

Bottom part of the dress (start in blue yarn)
Ch 20. Crochet in rows.
Row 1: start in second ch from hook, sc in next 5 st, hdc in next 14 st, ch 1, turn [19]
Row 2: work this row in BLO: hdc in next 14 st, sc in next 5 st, change to purple yarn, ch 1, turn [19]
Row 3: work this row in BLO: sc in next 5 st, hdc in next 14 st, ch 1, turn [19] (picture 13)

Row 4: work this row in BLO: hdc in next 14 st, sc in next 5 st, change to pink yarn, ch 1, turn [19]

Row 5: work this row in BLO: sc in next 5 st, hdc in next 14 st, ch 1, turn [19]

Row 6: work this row in BLO: hdc in next 14 st, sc in next 5 st, change to golden yarn, ch 1, turn [19]

Row 7: work this row in BLO: sc in next 5 st, hdc in next 14 st, ch 1, turn [19]

Row 8: work this row in BLO: hdc in next 14 st, sc in next 5 st, change to white yarn, ch 1, turn [19]

Row 9: work this row in BLO: sc in next 5 st, hdc in next 14 st, ch 1, turn [19]

Row 10: work this row in BLO: hdc in next 14 st, sc in next 5 st, change to blue yarn, ch 1, turn [19]

Row 11: work this row in BLO: sc in next 5 st, hdc in next 14 st, ch 1, turn [19]

Row 12: work this row in BLO: hdc in next 14 st, sc in next 5 st, change to purple yarn, ch 1, turn [19]

Repeat rows 3-12 two more times. Repeat rows 3-10 one more time but stop before the color change to blue yarn. You'll have 40 rows in total and the last row is made in white yarn.

Ch 1 and work in the row-ends of the top edge in white yarn (picture 14):

(sc in next 2 st, dec) repeat 10 times [30] (picture 15)

Fasten off, leaving a long tail for sewing. Sew the bottom part of the dress to the leftover front loops of row 5 of the upper part of the dress (pictures 16-17), then use the remaining yarn tail to sew both ends of the bottom part together (sew about 6 to 7 stitches closed). Fasten off and weave in the yarn end (picture 18).

UNDERSKIRT (in white yarn)

Ch 31. Work in joined rounds.

Rnd 1: start in second ch from hook, sc in next 30 st, slst in first st, ch 2 [30]

Rnd 2: (dc in next 4 st, dc inc in next st) repeat 6 times, slst in first st, ch 2 [36]

Rnd 3: (dc in next 5 st, dc inc in next st) repeat 6 times, slst in first st, ch 2 [42]

Rnd 4: (dc in next 6 st, dc inc in next st) repeat 6 times, slst in first st, ch 2 [48]

Rnd 5: (dc in next 7 st, dc inc in next st) repeat 6 times, slst in first st, ch 2 [54]

Rnd 6: (dc in next 8 st, dc inc in next st) repeat 6 times, slst in first st, ch 2 [60]

Rnd 7: (dc in next 9 st, dc inc in next st) repeat 6 times, slst in first st, ch 2 [66]

Rnd 8: BLO (dc inc in next st, ch 1) repeat 66 times, slst in first st.

Fasten off and weave in the yarn end (picture 19).

BOOT (make 2, start in golden yarn)

Ch 7. Stitches are worked around both sides of the

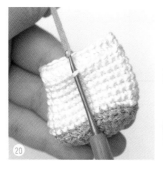

foundation chain.

Rnd 1: start in second ch from hook, inc in this st, sc in next 4 st, 4 sc in next st. Continue on the other side of the foundation chain, sc in next 4 st, inc in next st [16]

Rnd 2: (inc in next 2 st, sc in next 4 st, inc in next 2 st) repeat 2 times [24]

Rnd 3: (hdc in next st, hdc inc in next st) repeat 2 times, hdc in next 4 st, (hdc in next st, hdc inc in next st) repeat 4 times, hdc in next 4 st, (hdc in next st, hdc inc in next st) repeat 2 times, slst in next st, ch 1 [32]

Continue working in joined rounds.

Rnd 4: BLO sc in all 32 st, change to white yarn, slst in first st, ch 1 [32]

Rnd 5 – 6: sc in all 32 st, slst in first st, ch 1 [32]

Rnd 7: sc in next 9 st, (dec, sc in next 2 st) repeat 4 times, sc in next 7 st, slst in first st, ch 1 [28]

Rnd 8: sc in next 11 st, dec, sc in next 2 st, dec, sc in next 11 st, slst in first st, ch 1 [26]

Rnd 9: sc in next 9 st, dec, sc in next 4 st, dec, sc in next 9 st, slst in first st, ch 1 [24]

Rnd 10 – 11: sc in all 24 st, slst in first st, ch 1 [24]

Rnd 12: BLO hdc in all 24 st, slst in first st [24]

Fasten off and weave in the yarn end. Cut two strands of pink, blue, golden and purple yarn (approx. 2.5 in / 6 cm in length). Use the leftover front loops of round 11 and tie four strands (one of each color) on the right side of the right boot and the left side of the left boot (pictures 20-21).

UNICORN HEADBAND

Ear (make 2, in white yarn)

Rnd 1: start 6 sc in a magic ring [6]

Rnd 2: (sc in next st, inc in next st) repeat 3 times [9]

Rnd 3: (sc in next 2 st, inc in next st) repeat 3 times [12]

Rnd 4: (sc in next 3 st, inc in next st) repeat 3 times [15]

Rnd 5: (sc in next 4 st, inc in next st) repeat 3 times [18]

Rnd 6: (sc in next 5 st, inc in next st) repeat 3 times [21]

Rnd 7 – 8: sc in all 21 st [21]

Rnd 9: (sc in next 5 st, dec) repeat 3 times [18]

Rnd 10: sc in all 18 st [18]

Rnd 11: (sc in next 4 st, dec) repeat 3 times [15]

Slst in next st. Fasten off, leaving a long tail for sewing.

Horn (in golden yarn)

Rnd 1: start 6 sc in a magic ring [6]

Rnd 2: (sc in next st, inc in next st) repeat 3 times [9]

Rnd 3: sc in all 9 st [9]

Rnd 4: (sc in next 2 st, inc in next st) repeat 3 times [12]

Rnd 5: sc in all 12 st [12]

Rnd 6: (sc in next 3 st, inc in next st) repeat 3 times [15]

Rnd 7: sc in all 15 st [15]

Rnd 8: (sc in next 4 st, inc in next st) repeat 3 times [18]

Rnd 9: sc in all 18 st [18]

Rnd 10: (sc in next 5 st, inc in next st) repeat 3 times [21]

Rnd 11: sc in all 21 st [21]

Slst in next st. Fasten off, leaving a long tail for sewing.

Headband (in white yarn)

Ch 30. Crochet in rows.

Row 1: start in second ch from hook, sc in next 10 st, hdc in next 9 st, sc in next 10 st, ch 1, turn [29]

Row 2 – 3: sc in next 10 st, hdc in next 9 st, sc in next 10 st, ch 1, turn [29]

Row 4: sc in next 10 st, hdc in next 9 st, sc in next 10 st, ch 1, slst in last st of row 2 (picture 22).

Ch 36 to make the strap and fasten off. Pull up a loop of white yarn on the opposite side of row 2, ch 36 to make the second strap and fasten off. Stuff the horn with fiberfill and sew it in the center of the headband. Sew the ears on the headband, at approx. 2 stitches from the ends (picture 23).

HAIR (start in pink yarn, with a size C-2 / 2.75 mm crochet hook)

Note: You can either work the hair with the same crochet hook as the body (2 mm) and work more loosely, or you can work the hair with a bigger crochet hook (C-2 / 2.75 mm), as recommended.

Rnd 1: start 7 sc in the magic ring [7]

Rnd 2: inc in all 7 st [14]

Rnd 3: (sc in next st, inc in next st) repeat 3 times, inc in next 2 st, (sc in next st, inc in next st) repeat 3 times [22] Continue crocheting the hair strands.

Note: Strands 1-17 are made in the front loops of round 3 and strands 23-35 are made in the leftover back loops of the same stitches. Strands 18-22 are made in separate back loops of round 3.

Strand 1: ch 45 (picture 24), start in third ch from hook, hdc in next 13 ch, hdc inc in next ch, hdc in next 28 ch, sc in next ch (picture 25), slst in first front loop of Rnd 3 [44]

Strand 2: ch 14 (picture 26), start in second ch from hook, sc in next ch, hdc in next 11 ch, sc in next ch, slst in next front loop of Rnd 3 [13]

Strand 3 – 16: ch 45, start in third ch from hook, hdc in next 13 ch, hdc inc in next ch, hdc in next 28 ch, sc in next ch, slst in next front loop of Rnd 3 [44]

Strand 17: ch 14, start in second ch from hook, sc in next ch, hdc in next 11 ch, sc in next ch, slst in next front loop of Rnd 3 [13]

Strand 18: ch 45, start in third ch from hook, hdc in next 13 ch, hdc inc in next ch, hdc in next 28 ch, sc in next ch, slst in next back loop of Rnd 3 [44]

Strand 19 – 22: ch 14, start in third ch from hook, hdc in next 11 ch, sc in next ch, slst in next back loop of Rnd 3 [12]

Strand 23: ch 14, start in third ch from hook, hdc in next 11 ch, sc in next ch, change to purple yarn, slst in next back loop of Rnd 3 [12]

Strand 24: ch 45, start in third ch from hook, hdc in next 13 ch, hdc inc in next ch, hdc in next 29 ch, skip 1 ch, slst in next back loop of Rnd 3 [44]

Strand 25: ch 45, start in third ch from hook, hdc in next 13 ch, hdc inc in next ch, hdc in next 29 ch, change to pink yarn, skip 1 ch, slst in next back loop of Rnd 3 [44]

Strand 26 − 32: ch 45, start in third ch from hook, hdc in next 13 ch, hdc inc in next ch, hdc in next 28 ch, sc in next ch, slst in next back loop of Rnd 3 [44]

Strand 33: ch 45, start in third ch from hook, hdc in next 13 ch, hdc inc in next ch, hdc in next 28 ch, sc in next ch, change to blue yarn, slst in next back loop of Rnd 3 [44]

Strand 34 − 35: ch 45, start in third ch from hook, hdc in next 13 ch, hdc inc in next ch, hdc in next 29 ch, skip 1 ch, slst in next back loop of Rnd 3 [44]
Fasten off and weave in the yarn end (picture 27).

ASSEMBLY

- Sew the ears between rounds 72 and 76 of the head, at 6 stitches from the eyes.
- Embroider the eyebrows with dark brown embroidery thread at 3 stitches from the eyes. They should be 5 stitches wide.
- Embroider the nose with skin color yarn between rounds 59 and 60. The nose should be 4 stitches wide and can be made by passing the needle through 4 times.
- Embroider the lower 1/3 part of each eye with white yarn.
- Optionally, use pink make-up blush for the doll's cheeks.
- Sew on the hair. Sew or glue round 1 of the hair to the head. When positioning the hair strands, please note that the wrong side of the hair should point outward. Pin each hair strand into place using pins. Sew or glue each strand on (attach it until you reach the pin and leave the end of each strand

free). When using glue, pin each strand back down to dry (pictures 28-31).
  - Strand 17 is in front of the left ear and strand 2 is in front of the right ear.
  - Pin and sew strands 3-16 to the back of the head.
  - Strands 19-23 form the fringe.
  - Strands 24-35 form the upper layer of the hair.
  - Leave strand 1 between strands 2 and 23 and strand 18 between strands 17 and 19. Don't glue or sew these two strands.
- Tie the headband around the head and make a knot at the back.

Tayto
THE TROLL

A DESIGN BY LITTLEELLIES_HANDMADE (SARA BAILEY)

Tayto is a little troll who wants to find the most perfect and juicy mushrooms to take home and grow in his subterranean garden. He's very shy, but his love for mushrooms often gets him into a lot of trouble. Tayto is very good at hiding from the other big and scary trolls, to make sure he doesn't need to share his mushroom collection with anyone else.

Skill level: ★ (★)
Size: 10 in / 26 cm tall when made with the indicated yarn

Amigurumi gallery: Scan or visit www.amigurumi.com/4411 to share pictures and find inspiration.

YOU WILL NEED:

Light worsted weight yarn

- green
- beige
- white

Size B-1 / 2 mm crochet hook
Safety eyes (10 mm)
Yarn needle
Stitch markers
Fiberfill

HEAD (in green yarn)

Rnd 1: start 6 sc in a magic ring [6]
Rnd 2: inc in all 6 st [12]
Rnd 3: (sc in next st, inc in next st) repeat 6 times [18]
Rnd 4: (sc in next 2 st, inc in next st) repeat 6 times [24]
Rnd 5: (sc in next 3 st, inc in next st) repeat 6 times [30]
Rnd 6: (sc in next 4 st, inc in next st) repeat 6 times [36]
Rnd 7: (sc in next 5 st, inc in next st) repeat 6 times [42]
Rnd 8 – 13: sc in all 42 st [42]
Rnd 14: (sc in next 6 st, inc in next st) repeat 6 times [48]
Rnd 15: sc in next 7 st, inc in next st, sc in next 15 st, inc in next st, sc in next 7 st, inc in next st, sc in next 16 st [51]
Rnd 16: sc in all 51 st [51]
Rnd 17: sc in next 8 st, inc in next st, sc in next 13 st, inc in next st, sc in next 10 st, inc in next st, sc in next 17 st [54]
Rnd 18: sc in next 8 st, inc in next 3 st (mark the second inc with a stitch marker), sc in next 24 st, inc in next 3 st (mark the second inc with a stitch marker), sc in next 16 st [60]
Rnd 19: sc in next 11 st, inc in next st, sc in next 28 st, inc in next st, sc in next 19 st [62]
Rnd 20: (sc in next 29 st, dec) repeat 2 times [60]
Rnd 21: sc in all 60 st [60]
Rnd 22: (sc in next 8 st, dec) repeat 6 times [54]
Rnd 23: sc in next 9 st, dec, sc in next st, dec, sc in next 21 st, dec, sc in next st, dec, sc in next 14 st [50]
Rnd 24: (sc in next 3 st, dec) repeat 10 times [40]
Rnd 25: (sc in next 7 st, dec 2 times, sc in next 9 st) repeat 2 times [36]
Rnd 26: (sc in next 4 st, dec) repeat 6 times [30]
Rnd 27: (sc in next 3 st, dec) repeat 6 times [24]
Rnd 28: sc in all 24 st [24]

Fasten off, leaving a long tail for sewing. Stuff the head firmly with fiberfill.

BODY (in green yarn)

Rnd 1: start 6 sc in a magic ring [6]
Rnd 2: inc in all 6 st [12]
Rnd 3: (sc in next st, inc in next st) repeat 6 times [18]
Rnd 4: (sc in next 2 st, inc in next st) repeat 6 times [24]
Rnd 5: (sc in next 3 st, inc in next st) repeat 6 times [30]
Rnd 6: (sc in next 4 st, inc in next st) repeat 6 times [36]
Rnd 7: (sc in next 5 st, inc in next st) repeat 6 times [42]
Rnd 8: (sc in next 6 st, inc in next st) repeat 6 times [48]
Rnd 9: (sc in next 7 st, inc in next st) repeat 6 times [54]
Rnd 10 – 14: sc in all 54 st [54]
Rnd 15: (sc in next 7 st, dec) repeat 6 times [48]
Rnd 16: sc in all 48 st [48]
Rnd 17: (sc in next 6 st, dec) repeat 6 times [42]
Rnd 18 – 19: sc in all 42 st [42]
Rnd 20: (sc in next 5 st, dec) repeat 6 times [36]
Rnd 21 – 24: sc in all 36 st [36]
Rnd 25: (sc in next 4 st, dec) repeat 6 times [30]
Rnd 26 – 28: sc in all 30 st [30]
Rnd 29: (sc in next 3 st, dec) repeat 6 times [24]
Rnd 30: sc in all 24 st [24]

Fasten off and weave in the yarn end. Stuff the body firmly with fiberfill. Sew the head to the body.

EYE (make 2, start in white yarn)

Rnd 1: start 6 sc in a magic ring [6]
Rnd 2: inc in all 6 st [12]

Rnd 3: (sc in next st, inc in next st) repeat 6 times [18]
Rnd 4: (sc in next 2 st, inc in next st) repeat 6 times [24]
Rnd 5: (sc in next 3 st, inc in next st) repeat 6 times [30]
Change to green yarn.
Rnd 6: sc in all 30 st [30]
Rnd 7: BLO sc in all 30 st [30]
Fasten off, leaving a long tail for sewing.
Hold the eye with the opening away from you. Pull up a loop of green yarn in the first remaining front loop of round 6.
Decorative round 1: FLO sc in all 30 st [30]
Fasten off and weave in the yarn end.
Insert the safety eyes between rounds 2 and 3 of the eyes. Stuff the eyes lightly with fiberfill before sewing them to rounds 9-20 of the head, at 5 stitches from the stitch markers on the head. The eyes should touch each other in the middle. Make sure that the safety eyes are facing in the same direction.

NOSE (in green yarn)
Ch 3. Stitches are worked around both sides of the foundation chain.
Rnd 1: start in second ch from hook, inc in this st, 4 sc in next st. Continue on the other side of the foundation chain, inc in next st [8]
Rnd 2: (sc in next st, inc in next st) repeat 4 times [12]
Rnd 3: sc in all 12 st [12]
Fasten off, leaving a long tail for sewing. Stuff the nose with fiberfill and sew it between the eyes, on round 18.

EAR (make 2, in green yarn)
Rnd 1: start 6 sc in a magic ring [6]
Rnd 2: inc in all 6 st [12]
Rnd 3: (sc in next st, inc in next st) repeat 6 times [18]
Rnd 4: (sc in next 2 st, inc in next st) repeat 6 times [24]
Rnd 5: (sc in next 11 st, inc in next st) repeat 2 times [26]

Rnd 6 – 8: sc in all 26 st [26]
Rnd 9: sc in next st, (dec, sc in next 2 st) repeat 6 times, sc in next st [20]
Rnd 10 – 11: sc in all 20 st [20]
The ears don't need to be stuffed. Flatten the opening of the ear with the last stitch on the side and work the next round through both layers to close.
Rnd 12: sc in all 10 st [10] (picture 1)
Fasten off, leaving a long tail for sewing. Pinch the ears and join them with a stitch (picture 2). Sew the ears to rounds 12-13 of the head, aligned to the stitch markers on the head.

HORN (make 2, start in beige yarn)
Rnd 1: start 4 sc in a magic ring [4]
Rnd 2: sc in all 4 st [4]
Rnd 3: inc in next st, sc in next 3 st [5]
Rnd 4: sc in all 5 st [5]
Rnd 5: inc in next st, sc in next 4 st [6]
Rnd 6: inc in next st, sc in next 5 st [7]
Rnd 7: BLO sc in all 7 st [7]
Rnd 8: sc in next st, inc in next st, sc in next 4 st, inc in next st [9]
Rnd 9: sc in all 9 st [9]
Rnd 10: (sc in next 2 st, inc in next st) repeat 3 times [12]
Rnd 11: BLO sc in all 12 st [12]
Stuff the horn firmly with fiberfill and continue stuffing as you go.
Rnd 12 – 13: sc in all 12 st [12]
Change to green yarn.
Rnd 14: sc in all 12 st [12]
Rnd 15: BLO (sc in next 3 st, inc in next st) repeat 3 times [15]
Fasten off, leaving a long tail for sewing.
Hold the horn with the pointy end away from you. Pull up a loop of beige yarn in the first remaining front loop of round 6.

Decorative round 1: FLO sc in all 7 st [7]
Fasten off and weave in the yarn end.
Hold the horn with the pointy end away from you.
Pull up a loop of beige yarn in the first remaining front loop of round 10.
Decorative round 2: FLO sc in all 12 st [12]
Fasten off and weave in the yarn end.
Hold the horn with the pointy end away from you.
Pull up a loop of green yarn in the first remaining front loop of round 14.
Decorative round 3: FLO sc in all 12 st [12]
Fasten off and weave in the yarn end.
Sew the horns to rounds 4-9 of the head, above the ears. The horns should naturally curve downward after stuffing them.

TOOTH (make 2, in white yarn)
Ch 3. Stitches are worked around both sides of the foundation chain.
Rnd 1: start in second ch from hook, sc in this st, 3 sc in next st. Continue on the other side of the foundation chain, inc in next st [6]
Rnd 2: sc in all 6 st [6]
Fasten off, leaving a long tail for sewing. The teeth don't need to be stuffed.

MOUTH (in green yarn)
Ch 11. Crochet in rows.

Row 1: start in second ch from hook, sc in next 2 st, inc in next st, sc in next 4 st, inc in next st, sc in next 2 st, ch 1, turn [12]
Row 2: sc in next st, inc in next st, sc in next 8 st, inc in next st, sc in next st, ch 1, turn [14]

  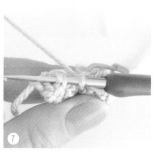 

Row 3: inc in next st, sc in next 12 st, inc in next st, ch 1, turn [16]

Row 4: sc in next 2 st, inc in next st, sc in next 10 st, inc in next st, sc in next 2 st, ch 1, turn [18]

Row 5: inc in next st, sc in next 16 st, inc in next st, ch 1, turn [20]

Work the next round around the mouth.

Rnd 6: sc in next 5 row-ends down the side, sc in next 10 st along the foundation chain, sc in next 5 row-ends up the other side, hdc in next 20 st along the top of the mouth [40] (pictures 3-4)

Fasten off, leaving a long tail for sewing. Pin the mouth beneath the nose, with the bottom of the mouth on the joining round of the head and body. Pin and sew the teeth on either side of the nose, they should protrude slightly from the mouth. Sew the mouth on.

FOOT (make 2, in beige yarn)

Big toe (make 2 for each foot)
Rnd 1: start 6 sc in a magic ring [6]
Rnd 2: inc in all 6 st [12]
Rnd 3 – 4: sc in all 12 st [12]
Rnd 5: (sc in next st, dec) repeat 4 times [8]
Rnd 6: sc in all 8 st [8]
Fasten off, leaving a yarn tail.

Little toe (make2 for each foot)
Rnd 1: start 6 sc in a magic ring [6]
Rnd 2 – 3: sc in all 6 st [6]
Fasten off on the first toe for each foot, leaving a yarn tail. Don't fasten off on the second toe.

Joining the toes
In the next round, we'll join the toes together to make the foot.

Rnd 4: sc in next 3 st on the second little toe, sc in next 3 st on the first little toe, sc in next 4 st on the first big toe, sc in next 8 st on the second big toe, sc in remaining 4 st on the first big toe, sc in remaining 3 st on the first little toe, sc in remaining 3 st on the second little toe [28]

Rnd 5: (sc in next 5 st, dec) repeat 4 times [24]
Sew the holes between the toes closed with the yarn tails. Stuff the toes and the foot with fiberfill and continue stuffing as you go.

Rnd 6: (dec, sc in next 2 st) repeat 6 times [18]
Rnd 7 – 9: sc in all 18 st [18]
Rnd 10: (sc in next st, dec) repeat 6 times [12]
Rnd 11: (sc in next st, dec) repeat 4 times [8]
Fasten off, leaving a yarn tail. Pull the yarn through the foot to sew it to the leg later.

LEG (make 2, start in beige yarn)
Rnd 1: start 6 sc in a magic ring [6]

Rnd 2: inc in all 6 st [12]

Rnd 3: BLO sc in all 12 st [12]

Rnd 4 – 6: sc in all 12 st [12]

Change to green yarn.

Rnd 7: (sc in next st, inc in next st) repeat 6 times [18]

Rnd 8: BLO (sc in next 2 st, inc in next st) repeat 6 times [24]

Rnd 9: sc in all 24 st [24]

Stuff the leg firmly with fiberfill and continue stuffing as you go.

Rnd 10: (sc in next 3 st, inc in next st) repeat 6 times [30]

Rnd 11: sc in all 30 st [30]

Fasten off, leaving a long tail for sewing.

Hold the leg with the opening toward you. Pull up a loop of green yarn in the first remaining front loop of round 7.

Decorative round: FLO sc in all 18 st [18]

Fasten off and weave in the yarn end. Sew the foot to the leg. Make sure the big toes on the feet are on the inside, toward the body. Use the yarn tail of the foot to sew it to the back loops of round 2 of the leg (picture 5). Make sure that the leg is positioned in the middle of the foot when sewing (picture 6).

HAND (make 2, in beige yarn)

Finger (make 4 for each hand)

Rnd 1: start 6 sc in a magic ring [6]

Rnd 2: sc in all 6 st [6]

Rnd 3: dec, sc in next 4 st [5]

Rnd 4: sc in all 5 st [5]

Fasten off on three fingers. Don't fasten off on the fourth finger.

Joining the fingers

In the next round, we'll join the fingers together to make the hand.

Rnd 5: sc in next 2 st on the fourth finger, sc in next 3 st on the third finger, sc in next 3 st on the second finger, sc in next 5 st on the first finger, sc in remaining 2 st on the second finger, sc in remaining 2 st on the third finger, sc in remaining 3 st on the fourth finger [20] (pictures 7-8)

Rnd 6: sc in all 20 st [20]

Stuff the fingers and the hand with fiberfill and continue stuffing as you go.

Rnd 7: (sc in next 8 st, dec) repeat 2 times [18]

Rnd 8: (sc in next 3 st, dec) repeat 2 times, dec 4 times [12]

Rnd 9 – 10: sc in all 12 st [12]

Change to green yarn.

Rnd 11: (sc in next 3 st, inc in next st) repeat 3 times [15]

Rnd 12: BLO sc in all 15 st [15]

Rnd 13 – 14: sc in all 15 st [15]

Rnd 15: dec, sc in next 13 st [14]

Rnd 16 – 17: sc in all 14 st [14]

Rnd 18: dec, sc in next 12 st [13]

Rnd 19 – 20: sc in all 13 st [13]

Rnd 21: dec, sc in next 11 st [12]

Don't stuff the next rounds.

Rnd 22 – 23: sc in all 12 st [12]

Rnd 24: dec 6 times [6]

Flatten the opening of the arm with the last stitch on the side and work the next round through both layers to close.

Rnd 25: sc in all 3 st [3]

Fasten off, leaving a long tail for sewing.

Hold the arm with the fingers away from you. Pull up a loop of green yarn in the first remaining front loop of round 11.

Decorative round: FLO sc in all 15 st [15] (picture 9)

Fasten off and weave in the yarn end.

Pin and sew the arms to round 28-26, diagonally on either side of the body, aligned with the stitch markers

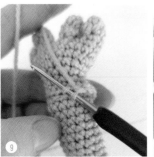   

on the head.

Pin and sew the legs between rounds 6 and 13 of the body, with an interspace of 10 stitches. Check to see if

your troll can sit without support. The arms should rest comfortably between the legs.

TAIL (in beige yarn)
Rnd 1: start 6 sc in a magic ring [6]
Rnd 2: inc in all 6 st [12]
Rnd 3 – 6: sc in all 12 st [12]
Rnd 7: (sc in next 2 st, dec) repeat 3 times [9]
Change to green yarn.
Rnd 8 – 24: sc in all 9 st [9]
Fasten off, leaving a long tail for sewing. Stuff the tail with fiberfill.
Cut strands of both green and beige yarn, approx. 3 in / 8 cm in length. Start with the beige strands. Insert your hook into a stitch of round 1, pull up a loop, pull the strand through the loop and pull tight to secure it (pictures 10-12). Work all the way around and down the tail and switch to green strands after round 6. Work green strands until you reach round 8 of the tail.
Sew the tail to the back of the body, between rounds 7 and 10.

Orion

THE CHIMERA

A DESIGN BY AMI TWINS DESIGN (MARIANA & MÓNICA)

Despite his big and fluffy mane, Orion is still a chimera cub. When he's not busy practicing his next set of flying exercises, he likes to dive into the kitchen and bake the most amazing cookies and cakes. Orion hopes he'll someday be able to take his best friends on a wild ride through the clouds.

Skill level: ★ ★ ★
Size: 5 in / 12 cm tall when made with the indicated yarn

Amigurumi gallery: Scan or visit www.amigurumi.com/4412 to share pictures and find inspiration.

YOU WILL NEED:

Fingering weight yarn
- orange
- brown
- beige
- purple
- lilac
- green (leftover)

Sport weight yarn
- light caramel
- dark caramel

Size B-1 / 2.5 mm crochet hook
Safety eyes (10 mm)
Yarn needle
Scissors
Pins
Stitch markers
Fiberfill
Wire brush

Note: Check your sport weight yarn colors to see if you can brush them with a wire brush. Some fibers may break when brushed.

HEAD (in orange yarn)

Rnd 1: start 8 sc in a magic ring [8]
Rnd 2: inc in all 8 st [16]
Rnd 3: (sc in next st, inc in next st) repeat 8 times [24]
Rnd 4: (sc in next 3 st, inc in next st) repeat 6 times [30]
Rnd 5: (sc in next 2 st, inc in next st, sc in next 2 st) repeat 6 times [36]
Rnd 6: (sc in next 5 st, inc in next st) repeat 6 times [42]
Rnd 7: (sc in next 3 st, inc in next st, sc in next 3 st) repeat 6 times [48]
Rnd 8 − 9: sc in all 48 st [48]
Rnd 10: (sc in next 7 st, inc in next st) repeat 6 times [54]
Rnd 11 − 18: sc in all 54 st [54]

Insert the safety eyes between rounds 11 and 12, with an interspace of 7 stitches. Make sure the start of the round is centered at the back of the head. Embroider a line around the side of each eye with green yarn (picture 1). Embroider the eyebrows with brown yarn in a diagonal line over 2 stitches, 2 stitches above each eye.

Rnd 19: (sc in next 7 st, dec) repeat 6 times [48]
Rnd 20: (sc in next 3 st, dec, sc in next 3 st) repeat 6 times [42]

Stuff the head with fiberfill and continue stuffing as you go.

Rnd 21: (sc in next 5 st, dec) repeat 6 times [36]
Rnd 22: BLO dec 18 times [18] (picture 2)
Rnd 23: (sc in next st, dec) repeat 6 times [12]
Rnd 24: dec 6 times [6]

Fasten off, leaving a yarn tail. Using your yarn needle, weave the yarn tail through the front loop of each remaining stitch and pull it tight to close. Weave in the yarn end

BODY (in orange yarn)

Pull up a loop of orange yarn in the last front loop of round 21 of the head (picture 3).

Rnd 1: FLO sc in all 36 st [36] (picture 4)
Rnd 2: (sc in next 5 st, inc in next st) repeat 6 times [42]
Rnd 3 − 10: sc in all 42 st [42]
Rnd 11: (sc in next 3 st, inc in next st, sc in next 3 st) repeat 6 times [48]
Rnd 12 − 13: sc in all 48 st [48]
Rnd 14: (sc in next 3 st, dec, sc in next 3 st) repeat 6 times [42]
Rnd 15: (sc in next 5 st, dec) repeat 6 times [36]
Rnd 16: dec 18 times [18]
Rnd 17: sc in all 18 st [18]
Rnd 18: dec 9 times [9]

Fasten off, leaving a yarn tail. Using your yarn needle,

weave the yarn tail through the front loop of each remaining stitch and pull it tight to close. Weave in the yarn end.

MUZZLE (in orange yarn)
Rnd 1: start 6 sc in a magic ring [6]
Rnd 2: inc in all 6 st [12]
Rnd 3: (sc in next 3 st, inc in next st) repeat 3 times [15]
Rnd 4: (sc in next 2 st, inc in next st, sc in next 2 st) repeat 3 times [18]
Rnd 5: sc in all 18 st [18]
Fasten off, leaving a long tail for sewing. Embroider the nose over rounds 3 and 4 with brown yarn. The nose is 3 stitches wide at the top. Mark the outline of the nose and then fill it in with vertical lines. Make a horizontal line on round 4 and a vertical line from round 3 to round 1 to finish. Sew the muzzle to the head, between the eyes, over rounds 12-17.

ARM (make 2, in orange yarn)
Rnd 1: start 6 sc in a magic ring [6]
Rnd 2: inc in all 6 st [12]
Rnd 3: (sc in next 3 st, inc in next st) repeat 3 times [15]
Rnd 4 – 6: sc in all 15 st [15]
Rnd 7: sc in next 2 st, dec 5 times, sc in next 3 st [10]
Rnd 8: sc in next 3 st, dec 2 times, sc in next 3 st [8]
Stuff the bottom of the arm with fiberfill and continue stuffing as you go, but stuff the top of the arm only lightly.
Rnd 9 – 12: sc in all 8 st [8]
Sc in next 2 st to reach the side of the arm, ch 1. Flatten the opening of the arm with the last stitch on the side and work the next round through both layers to close.
Rnd 13: sc in all 4 st [4]
Fasten off, leaving a long tail for sewing. Embroider 2 lines on the base of each arm with brown yarn to make the fingers. Sew the arms to the body between rounds 2 and 3, with an interspace of 1 stitch at the front (picture 5). Sew the lower part of the arms to the body, to secure them in place.

LEG (make 2, in orange yarn)

Rnd 1: start 6 sc in a magic ring [6]
Rnd 2: inc in all 6 st [12]
Rnd 3: (sc in next st, inc in next st) repeat 6 times [18]
Rnd 4 – 5: sc in all 18 st [18]
Fasten off, leaving a long tail for sewing. Sew the legs to the sides of the body, over rounds 9-14, at about 4 stitches from the arms (picture 6). Make sure you have enough space left to sew the feet on.

FOOT (make 2, in orange yarn)

Rnd 1: start 8 sc in a magic ring [8]
Rnd 2: (inc in next 3 st, sc in next st) repeat 2 times [14]
Rnd 3: (sc in next st, inc in next 3 st, sc in next 3 st) repeat 2 times [20]
Rnd 4 – 6: sc in all 20 st [20]
Rnd 7: (sc in next st, dec 3 times, sc in next 3 st) repeat 2 times [14]
Rnd 8: (dec 3 times, sc in next st) repeat 2 times [8]
Fasten off, leaving a long yarn tail. Using your yarn needle, weave the yarn tail through the front loop of each remaining stitch and pull it tight to close. Leave a long tail for sewing.

PAW PAD (make 2, in brown yarn)

Ch 4. Stitches are worked around both sides of the foundation chain.
Rnd 1: start in second ch from hook, sc in next 2 st, 3 sc in next st. Continue on the other side of the foundation chain, sc in next st, inc in next st [8]
Slst in next st. Fasten off, leaving a long tail for sewing. Sew the paw pad to the base of the foot. The top of the paw pad should cover the magic ring of the foot. Embroider 2 lines above the paw pad with brown yarn to make the toes. Sew the feet to the legs (pictures 7-8). Make a few stitches between the feet and the body as well to secure them.

TAIL (in orange yarn)

Rnd 1: start 6 sc in a magic ring [6]
Rnd 2 – 24: sc in all 6 st [6]
Fasten off, leaving a long tail for sewing.

FUR TAIL TIP (in light and dark caramel yarn)

Next, we'll make the furry tail tip using sport weight yarn. Cut approx. 24 yarn strands (approx. 5 in / 12 cm in length) in light and dark caramel.
Using your hook, pull a yarn strand through a stitch at the tip of the tail (picture 9-10). Then insert your hook through a stitch next to it and pull another yarn strand going through the loop you already made (picture 11). Pull the tail ends of the first strand, to tighten and secure (picture 12). Repeat this on rounds 1 to 4 of the tail. Alternate between light and dark caramel yarn in every stitch (we made the hair in round 4 in light caramel for a smoother result). Secure the last strand in

a previously added one. Use a wire brush to brush the yarn and trim it to the desired length. Sew the tail to the back, centered over rounds 13 and 14.

EAR (make 2, in orange yarn)
Rnd 1: start 6 sc in a magic ring [6]
Rnd 2: (sc in next st, inc in next st) repeat 3 times [9]
Rnd 3: sc in all 9 st [9]
Rnd 4: (sc in next 2 st, inc in next st) repeat 3 times [12]
Rnd 5: (sc in next 3 st, inc in next st) repeat 3 times [15]
Rnd 6: sc in all 15 st [15]
Fasten off, leaving a long tail for sewing. Pin the ears to the sides of the head, over rounds 4 to 8. Outline the mane using pins and a piece of brown yarn first. The outline pins (pictures 13-14) are placed as follows:
• between rounds 6 and 7, in the middle above the nose,
• between rounds 3 and 4, at 1 stitch from the previous pin,
• on each side next to the top of the ear,

• between rounds 9 and 10, at 4 stitches from the sides of the eyebrows.
The mane should come right in front of the ears, you can adjust the placement of the ears if needed. Sew the ears in place.
Also outline the mane at the base of the head, between rounds 19 and 20. You can weave a piece of yarn around the pins to visualize how the outline will look.

HORN (make 2, start in beige yarn)
Leave a long starting yarn tail on the outside of your piece.
Rnd 1: start 4 sc in a magic ring [4]
Rnd 2: inc in next st, sc in next 3 st [5]
Rnd 3: inc in next st, sc in next 4 st [6]

Rnd 4 – 5: sc in all 6 st [6]

Work the next rounds with alternating colors. You can use the jacquard technique. The color changes are indicated in italics.

Note: Don't crochet the slst too tightly, since you'll work in them in the next round.

Rnd 6: sc in next st, *(brown)* sc in next 4 st, *(beige)* sc in next st [6]

Rnd 7: sc in all 6 st [6]

Rnd 8: slst in next st, *(brown)* sc in next st, inc in next 2 st, sc in next st, *(beige)* slst in next st [8]

Rnd 9: slst in next st, sc in next 6 st, slst in next st [8]

Rnd 10: slst in next st, *(brown)* sc in next 2 st, inc in next 2 st, sc in next 2 st, *(beige)* slst in next st [10]

Stuff the horn lightly with fiberfill and continue stuffing as you go.

Rnd 11: slst in next st, sc in next 8 st, slst in next st [10]

Rnd 12: slst in next st, *(brown)* sc in next 3 st, inc in next 2 st, sc in next 3 st, (beige) slst in next st [12]

Rnd 13: slst in next 2 st, sc in next 8 st, slst in next 2 st [12] Slst in next st. This is the new end of the round.

Rnd 14: slst in next 2 st, *(brown)* sc in next 8 st, *(beige)* slst in next 2 st [12]

Rnd 15: slst in next 2 st, sc in next 8 st, slst in next 2 st [12]

Rnd 16: slst in next 2 st, *(brown)* sc in next 3 st, inc in next 2 st, sc in next 3 st, *(beige)* slst in next 2 st [14]

Rnd 17: slst in next 2 st, sc in next 10 st, slst in next 2 st [14] Slst in next st. This is the new end of the round.

Rnd 18: slst in next 2 st, *(brown)* sc in next 2 st, hdc in next 6 st, sc in next 2 st, *(beige)* slst in next 2 st [14]

Rnd 19: slst in next 2 st, sc in next 10 st, slst in next 2 st [14]

Rnd 20: slst in next 2 st, *(brown)* sc in next 2 st, hdc in next 6 st, sc in next 2 st, *(beige)* slst in next 2 st [14]

Rnd 21: slst in next 2 st, sc in next 10 st, slst in next 2 st [14]

Slst in next st. This is the new end of the round.

Rnd 22: slst in next 2 st, *(brown)* sc in next st, hdc in next 3 st, hdc inc in next 2 st, hdc in next 3 st, sc in next st, *(beige)* slst in next 2 st [16]

Fasten off the brown yarn and weave in the yarn end. Continue in beige yarn.

Rnd 23 – 24: sc in all 16 st [16]

Fasten off, leaving a long tail for sewing. Roll the tip of the horn to shape it in a spiral and use the starting yarn tail to sew it in place. Weave the yarn tail through the horn to secure the shape (picture 15). Sew the horns to rounds 6-11, behind the ears, tilted to the back of the head (picture 16).

MANE (in light and dark caramel yarn)

Next, we'll make the mane using sport weight yarn. Cut yarn strands (approx. 5 in / 12 cm in length) in light and dark caramel. About 2/3 of the mane is made in light caramel yarn and 1/3 is made in dark caramel yarn.

- Attach the yarn strands in the same way as the fur tail tip. Using light caramel yarn, work around the outline pinned on the face first and then work on the lower part of the mane at the base of the head, between rounds 18 and 19. When finishing a row,

secure the last strand in a previously added one.

- Now attach yarn strands in every stitch of the mane area. If you want more volume, you can attach yarn strands to every round of the head. If you want less volume, you can skip every 2 or 3 rounds at the back of the head.

- Make 1 row in light caramel yarn and 1 row by alternating light caramel and dark caramel yarn, and repeat. Don't add yarn between the ears and the horns, as it's hard to brush.

- Add one extra row at the front, between rounds 20 and 21, just below the line made between round 19 and 20.

- When you're finished attaching yarn (picture 17), you can brush the yarn strands. Brush 2 or 3 rows at a time and be careful not to brush the body. You can cover the body with a piece of paper to protect it while brushing the mane. Be extra careful around the horns, the ears and the front of the face.

- To finish, comb some strands in advance and attach them between the ears and the horns. Trim the mane to the desired length. You can also trim between layers to remove excess volume.

RIGHT WING (start in lilac yarn)

Ch 14. Crochet in rows. Work the entire wing in BLO.

Row 1: start in third ch from hook, hdc in next 4 st, sc in next 6 st, slst in next 2 st, ch 1, turn [12]

Mark the space below the last slst (on the side on the wing) with a stitch marker (picture 18).

Row 2: slst in next 2 st, sc in next 6 st, hdc in next 2 st, hdc dec, ch 2, turn [11]

Row 3: hdc dec, hdc in next st, sc in next 6 st, slst in next 2 st, ch 1, turn [10]

Row 4: slst in next 2 st, sc in next 6 st, hdc in next st, hdc inc in next st, ch 2, turn [11]

Row 5: hdc inc in next st, hdc in next 2 st, sc in next 6 st, slst in next 2 st [12]

Slst in the space marked with the stitch marker (don't remove the marker) (picture 19). Don't count this stitch, ch 1, turn and continue working into the last slst of row 5.

Row 6: slst in next 2 st, sc in next 6 st, hdc in next 2 st, hdc dec, ch 2, turn [11]

Row 7: hdc dec, hdc in next st, sc in next 6 st, slst in next 2 st, ch 1, turn [10]

Row 8: slst in next 2 st, sc in next 6 st, hdc in next st, hdc inc in next st, ch 2, turn [11]

Row 9: hdc inc in next st, hdc in next 2 st, sc in next 6 st, slst in next 2 st [12] (picture 20)

Slst in the space marked with the stitch marker and remove the marker. Don't count this stitch, ch 1, turn and continue working into the last slst of row 9.

Row 10: slst in next 2 st, sc in next 6 st, hdc in next 2 st, hdc dec, ch 2, turn [11]

Row 11: hdc dec, hdc in next st, sc in next 6 st, slst in next 2 st, ch 1, turn [10]

Row 12: slst in next 2 st, sc in next 6 st, hdc dec, ch 1, turn [9]

Row 13: dec, sc in next 5 st, slst in next 2 st, ch 1, turn [8]

Row 14: slst in next 2 st, sc in next 4 st, dec, ch 1, turn [7]

Row 15: dec, sc in next 5 st, ch 1, turn [6]

Row 16 – 17: sc in all 6 st, ch 1, turn [6]

Row 18: sc in all 6 st [6]

Fasten off, leaving a long tail for sewing.

Hold the wing with the front toward you and pull up a loop of purple yarn on the inside, at the top of the last row. Crochet around the wing as follows: sc in next 10 row-ends at the top, inc in the tip in the middle of the wing, sc in next 12 st across the foundation chain, work 1 extra sc in the corner (picture 21).

Fasten off and weave in the yarn end.

Crochet two lines with surface slst to make the wing branches. Work top down, over rows 5-6 and 9-10 of the wing (picture 22). You should have approx. 12 slst in each line.

LEFT WING (start in lilac yarn)

Ch 13. Crochet in rows. Work the entire wing in BLO.

Row 1: start in second ch from hook (mark the skipped chain with a stitch marker), slst in next 2 st, sc in next 6 st, hdc in next 4 st, ch 2, turn [12]

Row 2: hdc dec, hdc in next 2 st, sc in next 6 st, slst in next 2 st, ch 1, turn [11]

Row 3: slst in next 2 st, sc in next 6 st, hdc in next st, hdc dec, ch 2, turn [10]

Row 4: hdc inc in next st, hdc in next st, sc in next 6 st, slst in next 2 st, ch 1, turn [11]

Row 5: slst in next 2 st, sc in next 6 st, hdc in next 2 st, hdc inc in next st, ch 2, turn [12]

Row 6: hdc dec, hdc in next 2 st, sc in next 6 st, slst in next 2 st [11]

Slst in the chain marked with the stitch marker (don't remove the marker). Don't count this stitch, ch 1, turn and continue working into the last slst of row 6.

Row 7: slst in next 2 st, sc in next 6 st, hdc in next st, hdc dec, ch 2, turn [10]

Row 8: hdc inc in next st, hdc in next st, sc in next 6 st, slst in next 2 st, ch 1, turn [11]

Row 9: slst in next 2 st, sc in next 6 st, hdc in next 2 st,

hdc inc in next st, ch 2, turn [12]

Row 10: hdc dec, hdc in next 2 st, sc in next 6 st, slst in next 2 st [11]

Slst in the chain marked with the stitch marker and remove the marker. Don't count this stitch, ch 1, turn and continue working into the last slst of row 10.

Row 11: slst in next 2 st, sc in next 6 st, hdc in next st, hdc dec, ch 2, turn [10]

Row 12: hdc dec, sc in next 6 st, slst in next 2 st, ch 1, turn [9]

Row 13: slst in next 2 st, sc in next 5 st, dec, ch 1, turn [8]

Row 14: dec, sc in next 4 st, slst in next 2 st, ch 1, turn [7]

Row 15: sc in next 5 st, dec, ch 1, turn [6]

Row 16 – 17: sc in all 6 st, ch 1, turn [6]

Row 18: sc in all 6 st [6]

Fasten off, leaving a long tail for sewing. Hold the wing with the front toward you and pull up a loop of purple yarn on the outside, at the edge of the first row. Crochet around the wing as follows: inc in first st, sc in next 11 st across the foundation chain, inc in the tip in the middle of the wing, sc in next 10 row-ends across the top of the wing, work 1 extra sc in the corner. Fasten off and weave in the yarn end. Crochet two lines with surface slst to make the wing branches. Work top down, over rows 5-6 and 9-10 of the wing. You should have approx. 12 slst in each line (picture 22).

Sew the wings at the back of the body, between rounds 3 and 9, with an interspace of 11 stitches (picture 23). Sew the last 4 rows of each wing to the body for extra strength. The bushy mane will help to keep the wings in place as well.

Maisie
THE KRAKEN

A DESIGN BY AIRALI DESIGN (ILARIA CALIRI)

Maisie is the youngest kraken in the family, she's a sweet and friendly baby. Her playtime is spent with little colorful paper (ehm … crochet) boats, moving them around while dreaming of adventures in the ocean. Will she follow in her family's footsteps, destroying ships and dragging sailors to their doom? Maybe we'll see new — and peaceful — family traditions on the horizon.

Skill level: ★★
Size: 5.5 in / 14 cm tall when made with the indicated yarn

Amigurumi gallery: Scan or visit www.amigurumi.com/4413 to share pictures and find inspiration.

HEAD (in green yarn)

Rnd 1: start 6 sc in a magic ring [6]

Rnd 2: (sc in next st, inc in next st) repeat 3 times [9]

Rnd 3: (sc in next st, inc in next st, sc in next st) repeat 3 times [12]

Rnd 4: (sc in next st, inc in next st, sc in next st) repeat 4 times [16]

Rnd 5: (sc in next 3 st, inc in next st) repeat 4 times [20]

Rnd 6: (sc in next 2 st, inc in next st, sc in next 2 st) repeat 4 times [24]

Rnd 7: (sc in next 5 st, inc in next st) repeat 4 times [28]

Rnd 8: (sc in next 3 st, inc in next st, sc in next 3 st) repeat 4 times [32]

Rnd 9: (sc in next 7 st, inc in next st) repeat 4 times [36]

Rnd 10: (sc in next 4 st, inc in next st, sc in next 4 st) repeat 4 times [40]

Rnd 11: (sc in next 9 st, inc in next st) repeat 4 times [44]

Rnd 12: (sc in next 5 st, inc in next st, sc in next 5 st) repeat 4 times [48]

Rnd 13: (sc in next 11 st, inc in next st) repeat 4 times [52]

Rnd 14: (sc in next 6 st, inc in next st, sc in next 6 st) repeat 4 times [56]

Rnd 15 – 21: sc in all 56 st [56]

Rnd 22: slst in all 56 st [56]

Rnd 23: work in the sc of Rnd 21 (the slst of Rnd 22 sit at the front of the work), (sc in next 5 st, dec) repeat 8 times [48] (pictures 1-2)

Rnd 24: slst in all 48 st [48]

Rnd 25: work in the slst of Rnd 24, sc in all 48 st [48] (picture 3)

Rnd 26: sc in all 48 st [48] (picture 4)

Rnd 27: (sc in next 2 st, dec, sc in next 2 st) repeat 8 times [40]

Rnd 28: (dec, sc in next 3 st) repeat 8 times [32]

Rnd 29: sc in all 32 st [32]

Fasten off, leaving a long tail for sewing. Insert the safety eyes between rounds 25 and 26, with an interspace of 12 stitches (picture 5). With mint yarn, embroider a wide mouth between the eyes. Pass the

needle under the main stitch and wrap the yarn around to create a thicker mouth (picture 6).

CHEEK (make 2, in pink yarn)
Rnd 1: start 6 sc in a magic ring [6]
Fasten off, leaving a long tail for sewing. Sew the cheeks next to the eyes. Stuff the head with fiberfill.

LEG (make 8, in green yarn)
Rnd 1: start 6 sc in a magic ring [6]
Rnd 2: (inc in next st, sc in next 2 st) repeat 2 times [8]
Rnd 3: sc in all 8 st [8]

Rnd 4: inc in next 2 st, sc in next st, dec 2 times, sc in next st [8]
Rnd 5: (sc in next st, inc in next st) repeat 2 times, sc in next 4 st [10]
Rnd 6: (sc in next st, inc in next st) repeat 2 times, sc in next st, dec 2 times, sc in next st [10]
Rnd 7: sc in all 10 st [10]
Rnd 8: (sc in next 2 st, inc in next st) repeat 2 times, sc in next 4 st [12]
Rnd 9 – 11: sc in all 12 st [12]
Fasten off and weave in the yarn end on 7 legs. Don't fasten off on the 8th leg, sc in next 3 st to reach the side of this leg. The legs curl slightly outward and the last stitch of round 11 sits at the center back of the leg (picture 7). In the next round, we'll join the legs together to make the body.

BODY (continue in green yarn)
Rnd 12: sc in next 6 st on the 8th leg, (sc in next 6 st on the next leg) repeat 7 times [48] (pictures 8-9)
At the end of this round the 8 legs are joined together at the front, while 6 stitches at the back of each leg are free. We'll work on those stitches later to close the belly.

Rnd 13: sc in all 48 st [48]
Rnd 14: (sc in next 2 st, dec, sc in next 2 st) repeat 8 times [40]
Rnd 15: (dec, sc in next 3 st) repeat 8 times [32]
Rnd 16: slst in all 32 st [32]
Fasten off and weave in the yarn end (picture 10).

BELLY (in green yarn)
Hold the body upside down (picture 11), with the legs pointing slightly upward. Pull up a loop of green yarn between two legs (picture 12). In the next round, we work on the remaining 6 stitches of each leg.
Rnd 1: (sc in next 2 st, dec, sc in next 2 st) repeat 8 times [40] (picture 13)
Rnd 2: (dec, sc in next 3 st) repeat 8 times [32]
Rnd 3: (sc in next st, dec, sc in next st) repeat 8 times [24]
Rnd 4: (dec, sc in next st) repeat 8 times [16]
Rnd 5: dec 8 times [8]

Fasten off, leaving a yarn tail. Using your yarn needle, weave the yarn tail through the front loop of each remaining stitch and pull it tight to close. Weave in the yarn end (picture 14).
Stuff the legs lightly with fiberfill and stuff the body firmly with fiberfill. Sew the head to the body, with 3 legs positioned between the eyes (picture 15). Sew the small gaps between the legs closed with green yarn (picture 16).

HEAD FRILL (make 2, start in green yarn)
Ch 11. Crochet in rows.
Row 1: start in second ch from hook, inc in this st, sc in next 8 st, inc in next st, ch 1, turn [12]
Change to mint yarn. Fasten off the green yarn, leaving a long tail for sewing.
Row 2: sc in next st, hdc inc in next 10 st, sc in next st [22]
Fasten off and weave in the yarn end. Use the green yarn tail to sew the frills to the sides of the head,

between rounds 2 and 16 (pictures 17-18).

ARM (make 2, in mint yarn)
Rnd 1: start 6 sc in a magic ring [6]
Rnd 2: inc in next st, sc in next 5 st [7]
Rnd 3: sc in next 3 st, inc in next st, sc in next 3 st [8]
Rnd 4: inc in next st, sc in next 7 st [9]
Rnd 5: sc in next 4 st, inc in next st, sc in next 4 st [10]
The arm doesn't need to be stuffed. Flatten the opening of the arm with the last st on the side and work the next round through both layers to close.
Rnd 6: sc in next 2 st, slst in next st, ch 25, start in

second ch from hook, sc in next 24 back ridges of the ch, slst in same st as the previous slst, sc in next 2 st (picture 19).
Fasten off and weave in the yarn end. Sew the arms to the belly, next to the three legs at the front (picture 20). Embroider French knots on the head with mint yarn and make short straight embroidery stitches with yellow yarn.

BELLY COVER (in mint yarn)
Rnd 1: start 8 sc in a magic ring [8]
Rnd 2: inc in all 8 st [16]
Slst in next st. In the next round, we'll make an 8-pointed star shape to match the bottom of the belly and legs.
Rnd 3: (ch 10, start in second ch from hook, sc in next 6 ch, hdc in next 3 ch, skip 1 st on Rnd 2, slst in next st) repeat 8 times [8 points]

Rnd 4: (sc in next 9 st along the ch, inc in the tip, sc in next 9 st) repeat 8 times [160] (picture 21)
Fasten off, leaving a long tail for sewing. Weave in the yarn end if you are using sewing thread to sew it in place. Make French knots on rounds 3 and 4 of the belly cover with yellow yarn. Pin the belly cover in the middle of the belly. Sew the belly cover along the 8 points to the bottom of the belly and the legs, using mint sewing thread.

BOAT (in yellow yarn - or in any color of your choice)
Rnd 1: start 6 sc in a magic ring [6]
Rnd 2: (sc in next st, inc in next st, sc in next st) repeat 2 times [8]
Rnd 3: (sc in next 3 st, inc in next st) repeat 2 times [10]
Rnd 4: (sc in next 2 st, inc in next st, sc in next 2 st) repeat 2 times [12]
Rnd 5: sc in all 12 st [12]
The boat doesn't need to be stuffed. Flatten the opening of the piece with the last stitch on the side and work the next round through both layers to close (picture 22).
Rnd 6: sc in all 6 st, ch 1, turn [6]
In the next rounds, we work along the back and front loops of row 6 to start working in rounds again.

Rnd 7: work in BLO: inc in next st, sc in next 4 st, inc in next st). Rotate your work, work in remaining front loops: inc in next st, sc in next 4 st, inc in next st [16] (picture 23)
Rnd 8: (inc in next st, sc in next 6 st, inc in next st) repeat 2 times [20]
Rnd 9: (inc in next st, sc in next 8 st, inc in next st) repeat 2 times [24]
Rnd 10: sc in all 24 st [24]
Fasten off and weave in the yarn end (picture 24).
Fold rounds 9-10 outward.

Mae
THE SPRITE

A DESIGN BY CRITTER STITCH (STEPHANIE BUCKNER)

A cheeky little sprite, Mae is quite shy, but you may spot her from the corner of your eye when you walk in the forest. Mae loves tightrope walking and she'll often talk the tiny spiders of the forest into making extra threads for her to walk on. So if you spot any lonely spiderweb threads on your next walk, don't brush them away, Mae might just be using them for her balancing act.

Skill level: ★ ★
Size: 6 in / 15 cm when made
with the indicated yarn

Amigurumi gallery: Scan or visit
www.amigurumi.com/4414
to share pictures and find inspiration.

YOU WILL NEED:
Fingering weight yarn
- skin color of your choice
- light brown
- red
  white
Size B-1 / 2 mm crochet hook
Safety eyes (5 mm)
Black embroidery thread
Sewing needle
Pins
Stitch markers
Fiberfill
Optional: pink makeup blush

Note: The original sprite was made with a 0.90 mm crochet hook and lace weight yarn, she's really cute in this tiny size as well.

HEAD (in skin color yarn)

Rnd 1: start 6 sc in a magic ring [6]
Rnd 2: inc in all 6 st [12]
Rnd 3: (sc in next st, inc in next st) repeat 6 times [18]
Rnd 4: (sc in next 2 st, inc in next st) repeat 6 times [24]
Rnd 5: (sc in next 3 st, inc in next st) repeat 6 times [30]
Rnd 6: sc in all 30 st [30]
Rnd 7: (sc in next 4 st, inc in next st) repeat 6 times [36]
Rnd 8: sc in all 36 st [36]
Rnd 9: (sc in next 8 st, inc in next st) repeat 4 times [40]
Rnd 10 – 14: sc in all 40 st [40]
Rnd 15: (sc in next 8 st, dec) repeat 4 times [36]
Insert the safety eyes between rounds 11 and 12, with an interspace of 7 stitches. With black thread, embroider a small mouth 3 rounds below the eyes. The mouth should be 1 stitch wide.
Rnd 16: (sc in next 4 st, dec) repeat 6 times [30]
Rnd 17: (sc in next 3 st, dec) repeat 6 times [24]

Rnd 18: (sc in next 2 st, dec) repeat 6 times [18]
Rnd 19: (sc in next st, dec) repeat 6 times [12]
Fasten off, leaving a long tail for sewing. Stuff the head with fiberfill.

LEG (make 2, start in skin color yarn)

Rnd 1: start 6 sc in a magic ring [6]
Rnd 2: sc in all 6 st [6]
Rnd 3: (sc in next 2 st, inc in next st) repeat 2 times [8]
Rnd 4 – 5: sc in all 8 st [8]
Rnd 6: (sc in next 3 st, inc in next st) repeat 2 times [10]
Rnd 7 – 9: sc in all 10 st [10]
Rnd 10: (sc in next 4 st, inc in next st) repeat 2 times [12]
Stuff the leg with fiberfill and continue stuffing as you go.
Rnd 11 – 14: sc in all 12 st [12]
Rnd 15: (sc in next 5 st, inc in next st) repeat 2 times [14]

Rnd 16 – 17: sc in all 14 st [14]
Rnd 18: (sc in next 6 st, inc in next st) repeat 2 times [16]
Rnd 19 – 21: sc in all 16 st [16]
Change to white yarn.
Rnd 22: sc in all 16 st [16]
Fasten off and weave in the yarn end.

BODY (continue in white yarn)
Position the legs next to each other. In the next round
we'll join both legs together to make the body.
Rnd 1: insert your hook into one stitch of each leg,
pull up a loop of white yarn and join the legs with a
sc (picture 1), sc in next 15 st on the first leg, sc in
the connecting st (picture 2), sc in next 15 st on the
second leg [32] (picture 3)
Rnd 2: (inc in next st, sc in next 15 st) repeat 2 times [34]
Rnd 3: sc in next 3 st, inc in next, sc in next 10 st,
inc in next, sc in next 5 st, inc in next st, sc in next
10 st, inc in next, sc in next 2 st [38]
Rnd 4 – 5: sc in all 38 st [38]
Rnd 6: sc in next 4 st, dec, sc in next 26 st, dec,
sc in next 4 st [36]
Rnd 7: dec, sc in next 34 st [35] (picture 4)
Rnd 8: sc in all 35 st [35]
Rnd 9: dec, sc in next 33 st [34]
Rnd 10: sc in all 34 st [34]
Rnd 11: (dec, sc in next 7 st) repeat 2 times, (dec,
sc in next 6 st) repeat 2 times [30]
Rnd 12: sc in all 30 st [30]
Stuff the body with fiberfill and continue stuffing
as you go.
Rnd 13: (dec, sc in next 3 st) repeat 6 times [24]
Rnd 14 – 18: sc in all 24 st [24]
Rnd 19: (sc in next 5 st, dec 3 times) repeat 2 times,
sc in next 2 st [18]
Rnd 20: (sc in next 3 st, dec 3 times) repeat 2 times [12]
Change to skin color yarn.

Rnd 21 – 23: sc in all 12 st [12]
Rnd 24: dec 6 times [6]
Fasten off, leaving a yarn tail. Using your yarn needle,
weave the yarn tail through the front loop of each
remaining stitch and pull it tight to close. Weave in the
yarn end.

ARM (make 2, in skin color yarn)
Rnd 1: start 6 sc in a magic ring [6]
Rnd 2: (inc in next st, sc in next 2 st) repeat 2 times [8]
Rnd 3: inc in next st, sc in next 7 st [9]
Rnd 4: sc in all 9 st [9]
Rnd 5: dec, sc in next 7 st [8]

Rnd 6 – 17: sc in all 8 st [8]
Fasten off, leaving a long tail for sewing. The arms don't need to be stuffed.

DUNGAREES (in light brown yarn)

Dungarees legs (make 2)
Ch 18 and join with a slst to make a circle.
Rnd 1: sc in all 18 st [18]
Rnd 2: (sc in next st, inc in next st) repeat 9 times [27]
Fasten off and weave in the yarn ends.

Joining the dungarees legs
In the next round, we'll join the dungarees legs together.
Rnd 3: insert your hook into one stitch of each leg, pull up a loop of light brown yarn and join the dungarees legs with 4 sc through both legs (these 4 st don't count for the stitch total), sc in next 23 st on the first leg, sc in next 23 st on the second leg [46] (pictures 5-6)
Rnd 4: (sc in next 5 st, inc in next st) repeat 6 times, (sc in next 4 st, inc in next st) repeat 2 times [54]
Rnd 5 – 7: sc in all 54 st [54]
Rnd 8: (sc in next 7 st, dec) repeat 6 times [48]
Rnd 9: sc in all 48 st [48]
Rnd 10: (sc in next 6 st, dec) repeat 6 times [42]
Rnd 11: (sc in next 5 st, dec) repeat 6 times [36]
Rnd 12 – 13: sc in all 36 st [36]
Don't fasten off. Continue making the bib and the straps.

Bib and straps
Row 1: sc in next 24 st, ch 1, turn [24] (picture 7) Leave the remaining stitches unworked.
Note: Check to see if the bib is centered and add or remove stitches in row 1 if necessary.
Row 2: sc in next 9 st, ch 1, turn [9] Leave the remain-

ing stitches unworked.

Row 3 – 6: sc in next 9 st, ch 1, turn [9] (picture 8)

Row 7: sc in next 9 st, turn [9]

Row 8: ch 17, start in second ch from hook, sc in all 16 ch (picture 9), sc in next 7 st along the top of the bib (picture 10), ch 17, start in second ch from hook, sc in all 16 ch, slst in next st on the bib.

Fasten off and weave in the yarn ends. Sew the ends of the straps to the back of the dungarees (picture 11), put them on the doll first to see how the straps fit.

HAIR (in red yarn)

Rnd 1: start 6 sc in a magic ring [6]

Rnd 2: inc in all 6 st [12]

Rnd 3: (sc in next st, inc in next st) repeat 6 times [18]

Rnd 4: (sc in next 2 st, inc in next st) repeat 6 times [24]

Rnd 5: (sc in next 3 st, inc in next st) repeat 6 times [30]

Rnd 6: sc in next 2 st, (inc in next st, sc in next 6 st) repeat 4 times [34]

Rnd 7: sc in all 34 st [34]

Rnd 8: sc in next 2 st, (inc in next st, sc in next 7 st) repeat 4 times [38]

Rnd 9: (sc in next 8 st, inc in next st) repeat 4 times, sc in next 2 st [42]

Rnd 10 – 13: sc in all 42 st [42]

In the next round, we'll make the hair strands and the fringe.

Rnd 14: (slst in next st, ch 8, start in second ch from

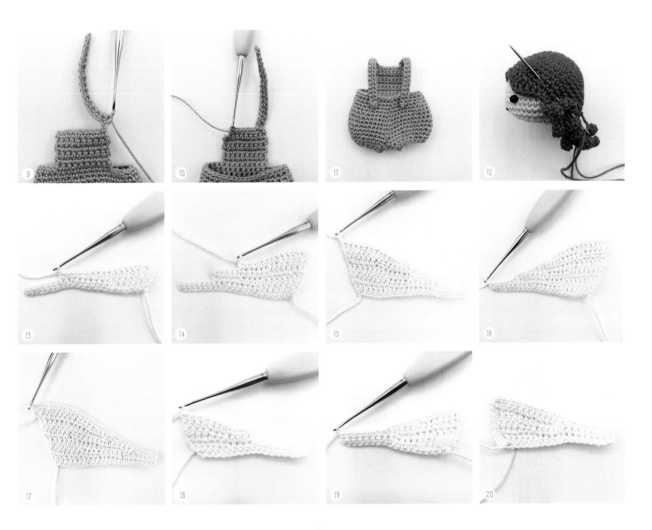

hook, sc in all 7 ch) repeat 10 times, dec, hdc in next 2 st, dc in next st, tr inc in next st, tr in next st, dc in next st, hdc in next st, ch 1, slst in next 2 st, ch 1, hdc in next st, dc in next st, tr in next st, tr inc in next st, dc in next st, hdc in next 2 st, dec, (slst in next st, ch 8, start in second ch from hook, sc in all 7 ch) repeat 11 times, slst in next st [21 + 21 strands] Fasten off, leaving a long tail for sewing. Sew the head to the body (make sure that two rounds of the neck are still showing). Optionally, you can add a bit of makeup blush on the cheeks. Place the hair on the

head and sew all around it (picture 12). Tie a piece of white yarn around the head to make a headband. Pin and sew the arms to the body, 2 rounds below the color change.

UPPER WING (make 2, in white yarn)

Ch 23. Crochet in rows.

Row 1: start in second ch from hook, sc in next 9 st, hdc in next 6 st, dc in next 6, dc inc in next st, ch 2, turn [23]

Row 2: dc inc in next st, dc in next 5 st, hdc in next 5 st, sc in next 5 st, ch 1, turn [17] Leave the remaining

stitches unworked. (picture 13)

Row 3: sc in next 5 st, hdc in next 5 st, dc in next 6 st, dc inc in next st, ch 2, turn [18]

Row 4: dc inc in next st, dc in next 4 st, hdc in next 4 st, sc in next 4 st, ch 1, turn [14] Leave the remaining stitches unworked (picture 14).

Row 5: sc in next 4 st, hdc in next 4 st, dc in next 5 st, dc inc in next st, ch 2, turn [15] (picture 15)

In the next row, we'll work all the way along the top side of the wing.

Row 6: dc inc in next st, dc in next 6 st, hdc in next 4 st, sc in next 4 st, dc in next st, hdc in next st, sc in next 3 st, dc in next st, hdc in next st, sc in next 5 st, ch 1, turn [28] (picture 16)

Row 7: sc in next 27 st, 4 sc in the corner st, sc in next 12 row-ends down the side of the wing, slst in next st [44]

Fasten off and weave in the yarn end (picture 17).

LOWER WING (make 2, in white yarn)

Ch 18. Crochet in rows.

Row 1: start in second ch from hook, sc in next 8 st, hdc in next 4 st, dc in next 4 st, 3 dc in next st, ch 2, turn [19]

Row 2: dc in next 3 st, hdc in next 3 st, sc in next 4 st, ch 1, turn [10] Leave the remaining stitches unworked.

Row 3: sc in next 4 st, hdc in next 3 st, dc in next 2 st, dc inc in next st, ch 1, turn [11] (picture 18)

In the next row, we'll work all the way along the top side of the wing.

Row 4: sc in next 11 st, dc in next st, hdc in next st, sc in next 7 st, ch 1, turn [20] (picture 19)

Row 5: sc in next 19 st, 4 sc in the corner st, sc in next 7 row-ends down the side of the wing, slst in next st [31] (picture 20)

Fasten off and weave in the yarn end.

21

Put the lower wing underneath the upper wing as shown in the picture and sew the top 5-6 stitches together (picture 21). Put the dungarees on and sew the wings to the back of the body, between the straps. Make sure the wings are positioned symmetrically and are pointing slightly downward.

THE TEAM OF DESIGNERS

Lex in Stitches (Alexa Templeton) — United Kingdom
Lex is an amigurumist, surgeon, and mother of two cheeky girls. She loves to play with color in her designs to create unique and joyful creatures.

Green Frog Crochet (Thuy Anh) — Vietnam
Thuy Anh fell in love with amigurumi in her first year of medical school. After graduation, she realized she loved yarn more than anything else in this world, so she chose to be a crocheter instead of a doctor. She's now a full-time mom and amigurumi designer, and loves what she's doing.

Airali Design (Ilaria Caliri) — Italy
Ilaria spends several hours of the day with a crochet hook and yarn in her hands. Amigurumi are her first and greatest love. After giving it a try, it's impossible to resist making these funny characters. Her books *'Amigurumi Winter Wonderland'* and *'Amigurumi Globetrotters'* are a paradise for crochet fans.

Blue Sparrow Handmade (Bianca Flatman) — Australia
Bianca works fulltime for an Australian airline and is often up in the middle of the night, giving her time to relax and crochet during the day. Blue Sparrow is a shared craft venture with her identical twin sister Mikala (who does lots of cool things with vinyl & digital svgs).

Amigurumeando con la Luna (Lúa Martinez) — Spain
Lua's interest in crochet was sparked by her great-grandmother, whom she remembers was always knitting and crocheting. Her own daughter Luna is her greatest inspiration, as she manages to bring out the best of her mom's creativity.

Petite Petals (Xue Ni Koh) — Malaysia/Indonesia
A lover of crafts and all things pretty and cute, Xue Ni learned to crochet through online tutorials. She found a world of creative freedom she quickly fell in love with, and began designing her own patterns. While she loves creating adorable amigurumi, she also enjoys the delicate art of lace crochet to make dainty miniature flowers.

DIY Fluffies (Mariska Vos-Bolman) — The Netherlands
When Mariska's sons leave for school and her husband goes off to work, she gets behind the sewing machine and picks up her crochet hook. With her boundless imagination, she makes the coolest patterns for stuffies! Her book *'Amigurumi Made Easy'* is the go-to crochet book for newbies to the craft.

Ami Twins Design (Mariana & Mónica Martins) — Portugal

Like most twins, Mariana and Mónica are all about teamwork, and that's how
Ami Twins came to be! Mariana prefers paint to yarn and loves to create new designs
for Mónica to bring to life with her crochet hook. Together, they join their skills to
bring their ideas to life and share them with anyone looking for a cozy friend.

Amour Fou (Carla Mitrani) — Argentina

Carla is a TV producer by day and a crochet addict by night. As
soon as the kids are off to bed, she enters her world of yarns and
hooks. She especially loves to make dolls she would have wanted
as a little girl herself.

MonsterHook (Anna Carax) — France

A passionate bookseller by day and a devoted crocheter in the
evening, Anna loves kawaii and cute-creepy designs inspired by
goth culture and metal music. Every day presents her with a new
opportunity to crochet.

AnaVicky Espiñeira — Argentina

Ana Vicky worked as a kindergarten teacher before
and loved creating toys for her little students.
Through time, creating cuddly worlds full of fantasy
has become her new favorite job.

Critter Stitch (Stephanie Buckner) — New Zealand / France

Stephanie is a Kiwi who lives in France. She loves anything
and everything creative, whether it's drawing, cooking,
embroidery, pottery, painting or crochet. Her love of nature
inspires her the most.

Littleellies_handmade (Sara Bailey) — United Kingdom

As a child, Sara loved teddy bears and took a bear with her everywhere
she went. When she realised she could make amigurumi bears for
herself, the passion for the craft really kicked in. With four children at
home, she makes almost anything their imaginations think up.

Our special thanks go to the fourteen designers who conjured up these wondrous creatures, to Studio Flits & Flash for the beautiful pictures, to the
proofreaders who carefully reviewed the patterns in this book (Ashton Kirkham, Jill Constantine, Kristi Randmaa, Serena Chew, Iris Dongo, Amanda
French, Barbara Roman, Debbie Eastman, Annegret Siegert, Shannon Kishbaugh, Luisa Willem, Marianne Rosqvist, Bianka Karolkiewicz, Lotte Nørgaard
Pedersen, Christina Fodero, Anna Persson, Karen Celestine Lee, Barbara Volcov, Sabine Schiffelhuber, Adrienn Weber, Silke Bridgman, Jimena Bouso,
Sandra Zheng, Louisa Wong, Dóra Sipos-Járási, Sandra Belleval and Mariska Van den Berg) and to all the fans who made this book possible.